5-Minute Faith Builders for Men

Bob Barnes

HARVEST HOUSE PUBLISHERS
EUGENE, OREGON

Cover by e210 Design, Eagan, Minnesota

Cover photo © iStockphoto / Rpsycho

5-MINUTE FAITH BUILDERS FOR MEN
Copyright © 2006 by Bob Barnes
Published 2012 by Harvest House Publishers
Eugene, Oregon 97402
www.harvesthousepublishers.com

Library of Congress Cataloging-in-Publication Data
Barnes, Bob, 1933-
  [Men under construction]
  5-minute faith builders for men / Bob Barnes.
     p. cm.
  Originally published: Men under construction. ©2006.
  ISBN 978-0-7369-3057-4 (pbk.)
  ISBN 978-0-7369-4198-3 (eBook)
  1. Christian men—Prayers and devotions. I. Title.
  BV4843.B374 2012
  248.8'42—dc23

                                                    2011032581

Printed in the United States of America

16 17 18 / BP-SK / 10 9 8 7 6 5

To you—the man reading this book

*Statistics tell us men don't read. Therefore,
you are to be complimented because you
break the stats. You're a reader!*

*And even more than a reader—you're a
man "under construction" who wants to
become more like Jesus. There are many
ways this can happen, but one of the major
ways I've found is through a willingness
to read, to apply, and to grow.*

*So my prayer is that as you read
5-Minute Faith Builders for Men you'll
be built by the Spirit of God into a better
man—and if you're married, a better husband,
and if you're a dad, a better father—and
more conformed to the image of Jesus Christ.*

May these daily nuggets enrich your life.

Daily Thoughts
to Build You Up

believe God is at work among men in America as well as
around the world in a mighty way. More and more men
are hearing and responding to His call to be leaders in the
family and the church.

Many men are naming Jesus as their Lord and Savior for
the first time, and others are rededicating themselves to the
Lord. If these commitments are to make a significant impact
in our families, our nation, and our world, they need to be
nourished daily—and that, I pray, is where this book of devotions will be helpful.

One way we sustain our commitment to the Lord is to
read His Word daily. Each of the readings in *5-Minute Faith
Builders for Men* is therefore designed to encourage you in your
spiritual journey by helping you understand what God's Word
has to say to you.

Each reading will start with a passage of Scripture and a short devotion based on what you've read. Then you'll pray about what you've read and be uplifted by an inspiring thought entitled "Today's Wisdom." Finally, you'll be challenged to act on what you've learned. James 1:22 encourages us to not only be hearers of God's Word, but to go one step further and be *doers* also. We must put God's Word into action.

Don't worry about reading the book from front to back. Skip around if you like. At the top of the first page of each reading, you'll find three boxes ❏ ❏ ❏. Put a checkmark in one of the boxes each time you read that devotion. In this way you can keep track of those devotions you've previously read.

May the Lord richly bless you as you listen for and respond to His call to you to be a leader in your family, your church, and your community.

Making Big
Choices of Life

*If any of you lacks wisdom, let him
ask of God, who gives to all men
generously and without reproach,
and it will be given to him.*

JAMES 1:5

*Our world is full of men who have
an abundance of knowledge, but there
are few of us who have wisdom.
Knowledge is horizontal. Wisdom is
vertical—it comes down from above.*

BILLY GRAHAM

have found that any wisdom I may have is that which I
have gained from the holy Scriptures. Anything else would
be counted as knowledge. Knowledge is much easier and faster
to acquire than wisdom. Gaining wisdom is a lifelong pursuit
and cannot be attained in a college class or through a search
on the Internet.

The Bible is full of wonderful assurances and promises
for all who believe in Jesus Christ, the Son of God. But each
person must accept Jesus as his own Savior before he can claim
these promises personally. How can these promises be yours?
The Bible says that you must—

- *Recognize* you cannot be saved by trying to be good,
  or because you are doing the best you can, or because you are a member of a social or religious

organization. God says we are not saved by our good works.

> By grace you have been saved through faith; and that not of yourselves, it is the gift of God; not as a result of works, that no one should boast (Ephesians 2:8-9).

• *Confess* that you cannot save yourself, that you are a guilty sinner worthy of God's righteous judgment, and that you are hopelessly lost without the Lord Jesus Christ as your personal Savior.

> If you confess with your mouth Jesus as Lord, and believe in your heart that God raised Him from the dead, you shall be saved; for with the heart man believes, resulting in righteousness, and with the mouth he confesses, resulting in salvation (Romans 10:9-10).

• *Believe* the good news that Jesus died for the ungodly (Romans 5:8). He also died for you and settled your sin debt by His death on Calvary's cross. Believe the blessed news that Christ was raised from the dead and now lives to save all who will come to Him in faith.

> He [Jesus] is able to save forever those who draw near to God through Him, since He always lives to make intercession for them (Hebrews 7:25).

• *Call* on the name of the Lord Jesus Christ with a sincere desire to be saved from your sins. God has promised that "whosoever shall call upon the name of the Lord shall be saved (Romans 10:13 KJV).

- *Rely* upon God's sure promise, not upon your feelings. By faith declare you are saved by the blood of Jesus Christ, shed for the forgiveness of your sins. Openly confess Him as your Lord and Savior.

> God so loved the world, that He gave His only begotten Son, that whoever believes in Him should not perish, but have eternal life (John 3:16).

If you have never put your faith in Jesus as your personal Savior, I encourage you to do it right now in the quietness of your own heart.

 ## Prayer

Father God, I realize I'm a sinner and separated from You. I open my heart to receive You as my personal Savior and Lord. I know You will forgive me of my sins. I want You to be my mentor and to give me guidance and purpose for life. I want You to be the Potter, and I will be the clay. Mold me and make me in Your own way. Amen.

 ## Action

Settle your status with Jesus. Confessing your sins, invite God into your heart.

 ## Today's Wisdom

"I went to Africa that I might be able to sin to my heart's content. I was a wild beast on the coast of Africa till the Lord caught and tamed me."

JOHN NEWTON

Handling Small Things in a Big Way

It is better to have little and be godly
than to own an evil man's wealth; for the
strength of evil men shall be broken, but the
Lord takes care of those he has forgiven.

PSALM 37:16–17 TLB

When we come to the Lord, He wants all of us, not just a bit here and a bit there. When we are new believers we aren't sure if we can trust this God in our lives. After all, we have no previous track record, and we're not sure He is capable of doing all He says He can do. So we give Him a little of this and a little of that, but that's not going to "cut the mustard." As we grow, we learn that God is asking more of us than we may have previously thought. Our faith is more than just a Sunday kind of faith.

In the following story, an Alcoholics Anonymous patron tells of his experience in giving to God all He asks for:

> After falling off the wagon and after sobering up, my sponsor told me I had to be willing to change everything about my life—everything! So, I wore blue jeans before and I switched to a nice pair of slacks. I previously wore Western shirts and I

switched to a plaid, collared, buttoned-up-the-front long-sleeve shirt. But the one thing I just couldn't give up was my cowboy boots.

I softly went to my sponsor and said in a very gentle fashion, "Surely I won't get drunk over a silly pair of cowboy boots. I'm willing to change a lot of things, and if needed I could even give up those boots, but it seems so silly."

My good-ol'-boy sponsor said, "I don't know how silly it is or if you'll get drunk over those cowboy boots, but I can tell you are not 'entirely' willing, though."

"Okay, okay," I said. "I'll prove it to you. I'll give up the boots for 30 days just to demonstrate my willingness to God." So I bought a pair of tennis shoes, and after 30 days of not wearing my boots, the strangest thing happened—my feet stopped hurting.

That's how it was getting sober and giving up the fast track of life. I never stopped to think that the boots were causing my feet to hurt, or the booze was causing my life to hurt. I got willing to give up the stuff, one day at a time, for 30 days, then 60 days, then 90 days…and my life stopped hurting.

Every day I do something different. Some change in some small way occurs in my life. Maybe I just put my socks on in a different fashion or drive to work in a new way. Every day I try to do little things in a big way so that when big things happen I can handle them in a little way.[1]

Who would have thought that a change in shoes would make such a difference? Is God asking you to change shoes? If not that, what? Each of us is being nudged by God to make a change. Not until we say "yes" to God are we going to get some relief from our pain. We must be willing to change our boots.

Prayer

Father God, if You tell me to change boots I'm willing and ready to change. I know that You have my good in front of You. I trust You with my life. I want to be the man You want me to become. Amen.

 Action

Ask God what boots He wants you to surrender…and then go buy a new pair of "tennis shoes"—that is, take off what God has asked you to let go of and take hold of what He has asked you to pick up.

 Today's Wisdom

Say "no" to good things and save your "yeses" for the best.

The Changing Phases of Dad

*Fathers, do not provoke your children
to anger; but bring them up in the
discipline and instruction of the Lord.*

EPHESIANS 6:4

It's amazing how the images of fathers change over a lifetime. I can remember with loving pride when my son, Brad, said as a little boy, "I want to be just like you, Dad." An insightful writer put together this list of comments:

- *age 4:* "My Daddy can do anything!"

- *age 7:* "My Dad sure knows a lot, a whole lot!"

- *age 8:* "My Dad doesn't know quite everything!"

- *age 12:* "Oh, well—naturally, my Dad doesn't know that either."

- *age 14:* "Oh, Dad? He's just out of date—he's old-fashioned."

- *age 21:* "Oh, that guy—he's sure not with it."

- *age 25:* "Dad? Well, he does know a little about it."

- *age 35:* "Before we decide what to do, we'll talk to Dad and get his ideas first."

- *age 50:* "I wonder what Dad would have thought about that."

- *age 60:* "My dad knew something about literally everything!"

- *age 65:* "I really wish I could talk it over with Dad just once more!"

If you're a father whose kids are at that stage of life (possibly their teenage years) when they don't quite think Dad is the coolest guy around, let me be an encouragement to you. That phase will soon pass, and Dad will become popular again.

Continue to love them and support them in prayer. They especially need your love during those times when they seem least like they deserve it. They will eventually grow wise and return to you with their questions about life. Just continue to be there for them.

Thank God along the way for grandchildren, for they will think you are the wisest man they know. Don't feel disappointed because your children don't appreciate you now. That's just part of their growing up and wanting to get out on their own. It's all part of cutting the cord. Don't let their negative words cripple you in your growth as a dad.

Those positive words will return again.

 Prayer

Father God, help me realize that my children will go through these sometimes difficult phases of life. Give me the courage to be the dad You would like for me to be—even when I may feel discouraged. May You be near to my children as they go through these cycles of life. Amen.

Action

If your dad is still alive, call or write him and tell him how much you appreciated his wisdom over the years. If he is no longer with you, write him a letter, just as if he were still alive, and thank him for being your dad.

Today's Wisdom

"Love does not need proof...it needs practice."

ROBERT STRAND

My life is a listening. His is a speaking.
My salvation is to hear and respond. The
sacrifice that pleases God is the offering
of my soul…entirely attentive to Him.

THOMAS MERTON,
Thoughts in Solitude

God's Man
for Life

*Through all this Job did not sin
nor did he blame God.*

JOB 1:22

landholder, rancher, and community leader, Job was the most respected and influential individual in the entire region. Still, his number-one priority was his large, active family. Despite the tremendous demands on him, he always had time for his children. They were never an interruption. And I'm sure you couldn't talk to him very long without his pulling from his wallet a favorite picture of his troop. He was always eager to tell you about each of them. This wise man knew that his only legacy of significance would be not his possessions or his bank accounts but his sons, his daughters, and his grandchildren. A man living in the present but with a vision for the future, a man of God, and a man whom God had greatly blessed, Job caught Satan's eye.

In Job 1:8, as the Lord holds court in the heavenlies, He asks Satan, "Have you considered my servant Job? There is no one on earth like him; he is blameless and upright, a man who fears God and shuns evil" (NIV).

Satan shrugs his shoulders and replies in effect, "Of course Job is close with You. Who wouldn't be? He's got all the advantages. You handle him softly and protect him. Just try taking away a few of his precious toys and then see what he does. He'll surely curse You to Your face."

For reasons unknown to us, God gives Satan some freedom to do what he wishes most, and that is to test Job's faith. God sets limits, but even within those limits Satan brings great loss and immeasurable pain to Job.

In a quick series of catastrophes, Job loses his business, his wealth, his health, and all ten of his children. At this point, Job's wife tells him to curse God and die (Job 2:9). In the midst of such devastation, would Job remain a man of God, or would he reject the God who had once so richly blessed him? Is Job a man of character or merely a fair-weather follower of God?

As the rest of the book of Job unfolds, we see that Job remains God's man and, by doing so, offers us many valuable lessons for life. One of these lessons is that though things on the outside can be taken away from us, no one can take away those things on the inside—our heart, our character, our soul. We can only lose these by throwing them away—by turning from God and following after false gods—but no one can ever rob us of a heart and soul committed to the Lord or of the character that results from that commitment.

So what will you do when the things of life are taken away from you? What will happen to your inner man? Will you stand strong in Christ? Will the loss purify and strengthen your character, or will hard times break you?

We know Job's trials strengthened his character, and people still talk about the patience of Job. But he demonstrated more than patience. He shows us a faith in God that has staying power and is able to endure to the end.

As our key verse says, "Through all of this [his losses and suffering] Job did not sin nor did he blame God." Now turn to Job 42:10-16 and see how our faithful God responds to His people who have faith in Him. May that passage give you hope when the circumstances of life bog you down. You can rejoice in the Lord in all situations and give thanks whatever challenges come your way, knowing that God is your faithful Redeemer.[2]

 Prayer

Father God, thank You for all You can teach me through the life of Job. Thank You for showing me the importance of faith that has staying power. May my life reflect the endurance of Job, whatever comes my way. Amen.

 Action

Think about specific struggles you've passed through and how you responded. Was your faith strengthened, or was a weakness of faith revealed?

 Today's Wisdom

Whether we succeed or fail from the world's point of view, God uses every circumstance to further His plans for our lives.

One good man who does not put on his religion once a week with his Sunday coat, but wears it for his working dress, and lets the thought of God grow into him…that man is worth a thousand sermons—he is a living Gospel….Men see his good works, and admire them in spite of themselves…and see that God's grace is no dream, but that the Holy Spirit is still among men…So they get a glimpse of God again in His saints and glorify their Father who is in heaven.

CHARLES KINGSLEY

It All Starts at Home

Children are a gift of the LORD;
the fruit of the womb is a reward.

PSALM 127:3

In a recent Bible study my wife, Emilie, and I attended, the teacher asked, "Did you feel loved by your parents when you were a child?" The answers were disturbing and, for us parents, quite convicting. Here were some of the responses:

- "Dad took us on trips, but he played golf all the time we were away."

- "Mom was too involved at the country club to spend time with us."

- "They were too busy for me."

- "A lot of pizzas were delivered to our house on Friday nights when my parents went out for the evening."

- "I spent too much time with the babysitters."

- "I got in their way. I wasn't important to them."

- "Mom didn't have to work, but she did so she wouldn't have to be home with us children."

What do you think your children would say if someone asked them, "Do you feel loved by your parents?" Which of your actions would support their answer, positive or negative?

Psalms 127:1–128:4 gives us some principles for building a family in which children are confident that their parents love them. First, the psalmist addresses the foundation and protection of the home:

> Unless the LORD builds the house, its builders labor in vain. Unless the LORD watches over the city, the watchmen stand guard in vain (127:1 NIV).

In the Old Testament, the protective wall surrounding a city was the very first thing to be constructed when a new city was built. The Israelites knew they needed protection from the enemy, but they were also smart enough to know even their stout walls could be climbed over, knocked down, or broken apart. They realized their ultimate security was the Lord standing guard over the city.

Are you looking to God to help you build your home? Are you trusting the Lord to be the guard over your family? Many forces in today's society threaten your family. When we drive the Southern California freeways, we see commuting parents who are burning the candle at both ends to provide for all the material things they think will make their families happy—but often at the expense of *time* with their children.

We rise early and retire late, but Psalm 127:2 tells us that these efforts are futile. We are to do our best to provide for and protect our family, but we must trust first and foremost in God to take care of them.

In verse 3 we read that "children are a reward [gift] from [the Lord]." In the Hebrew, *gift* means *property, possession.*

Truly God has loaned us our children to care for and to enjoy for a certain period of time. They remain His property, His possessions. As stewards of our children we are to take care of them—and that takes time.

I love to grow vegetables each summer and am always amazed at what it takes to get a good crop. I have to cultivate the soil, sow the seeds, water, fertilize, weed, and prune. Raising children takes a lot of time, care, nurturing, and cultivating too. We can't neglect these responsibilities if we are going to produce good fruit. Left to themselves, our children—like the garden—will fail to bear fruit and will grow, if anything, only weeds. When I *do* tend the garden, however, I'm rewarded by corn, tomatoes, cucumbers, and beans. Just as the harvest is my reward, so God-fearing children are a good parent's reward.

Next, Psalm 127:4-5 compares children to arrows in the hands of a warrior, and talks about how parents are to handle their offspring. Wise and skillful parents will know their children, understand them, and carefully point them in the right direction before shooting them into the world. And, as you may have learned in an archery class, shooting an arrow straight and hitting a target is a lot harder in real life than it looks like in the movies or on TV. Likewise, godly and skillful parenting isn't easy.

Critical to success as a parent is the acknowledgment of the Lord's presence in the home:

- The Lord is central to a home's happiness (Psalm 128:1-2).

- A wife who knows the Lord will be a source of beauty and life in the home (verse 3a).

- With the Lord's blessing, children will flourish like olive trees, which generously provide food, oil, and shelter for others (verse 3b).

Ask yourself, *What can I do to make the Lord's presence more recognizable in my home?*

Finally, to ask a more pointed question, what kind of steward am I being in my home? God has entrusted to you some very special people—your children. You will be held accountable for how you take care of them. But you're not in this job alone. God offers guidelines like those we looked at today plus His wisdom and His love to help you do the job and do it well.[3]

 ## Prayer

Father God, forgive me for the ways I shortchange my children. Help me know how to slow down the pace of life. Help me stay very aware that my children will be with me for just a short time, and that how I treat them will affect them and their children's lives too. Continue to teach me how to be the parent You want me to be. Amen.

 ## Action

Give your child/children the gift of time—today and every day.

 ## Today's Wisdom

"The Christian home is the Master's workshop, where the processes of character-molding are silently, lovingly, faithfully, and successfully carried on."

RICHARD M. MILNES

A Piece of Cake

*We know that God causes all things
to work together for good to those
who love God, to those who are
called according to His purpose.*

ROMANS 8:28

Have you ever asked the question, "Why me, Lord?"

When my wife, Emilie, was first diagnosed with cancer, we had all kinds of questions cross our mind. However, from past experience in difficult situations we knew that nothing comes to us before it first comes through God. Without a doubt we knew all things work together for good. The secular world doesn't know or understand that principle. As believers, though, we can be at peace when trials come our way.

I once heard a great explanation when someone asked, "What did I do to deserve this?" Here's the story:

> A daughter is telling her mother how everything is going wrong in her life. She is failing algebra, her boyfriend has broken up with her, and her best friend is moving away.
>
> As the mother listens, she's baking a cake. When she asks her daughter if she would like a snack,

the daughter says, "Absolutely, Mom—I love your cake."

"Here, have some cooking oil," her mother offers.

"Yuck!"

"How about a couple raw eggs?"

"Gross, Mom!"

Her mother replied, "Would you like some flour then? Or maybe baking soda?"

"Mom, those are all yucky!"

To which the mother replies, "Yes, all those things seem bad all by themselves, but when they are put together in the right way, they make a wonderfully delicious cake! Life works the same way."[4]

Sometimes we wonder why God lets us go through such bad and difficult times. But God knows that when He puts these things all in His order, they always work for good. We just have to trust Him—and eventually, they will all make something wonderful!

 Prayer

Father God, life isn't always a piece of cake, but when we let You mold us into Your kind of cake we will be delicious to the taste. You always put in the right amount of ingredients to make us perfect. Help me trust You in everything. Amen.

 Action

Stop by a bakery or grocery store today (maybe on your way home from work) and buy a special cake for dessert tonight. Share this story with your family as you enjoy the treat!

 ## Today's Wisdom

"God is crazy about you. He sends you flowers every spring and a sunrise every morning. Whenever you want to talk, He'll listen. He can live anywhere in the universe, and He chose your heart. I hope your day is a 'piece of cake.'"

AUTHOR UNKNOWN

When Bad Times Roll

*God is our refuge and strength, always
ready to help in times of trouble. So we
will not fear, even if earthquakes come
and the mountains crumble into the sea.*

PSALM 46:1-2 NLT

On December 26, 2004, the world was shocked to hear that a 9.0 earthquake in the ocean off southeast Asia had caused a mighty tsunami to crash ashore in several countries and destroy entire towns, with the death toll at well over 200,000.

People cried out, "Where are You, God? How could You let this happen?"

We always ask this "why" question at such times. Our inquiring minds want to know. *Why* would a loving God permit such death, particularly when the toll included many children?

The sad fact is, we live in a fallen world, and events happen according to the laws of nature. Because of the sin of mankind there will always be things that happen other than what we would want—a perfect world. There will be troubles and suffering beyond our control. At such times, our comfort must come from God's Word.

In today's verse we find three comforts in such events of life:

- God is our refuge.
- God is our strength.
- God is always ready to help in times of trouble.

If we can internalize these "big three" promises we can live with this victory:

- We will not live in fear.

What great assurance when our soul quakes. We can apply these promises to all events of life—tsunamis, earthquakes, heartbreaks, or soul quakes.

Just remember, when we walk through life's storms we have two alternatives:

1. respond as a faith-filled person
2. respond as a faithless person

> How blessed is the man who does not walk in the counsel of the wicked, nor stand in the path of sinners, nor sit in the seat of scoffers! But his delight is in the law of the LORD, and in the law he meditates day and night, and he will be like a tree firmly planted by streams of water, which yields its fruit in its season, and its leaf does not wither; and whatever he does, he prospers (Psalm 1:1-3).

A faith-filled man will respond in these ways:

- He delights in reading and knowing God's Word.
- He meditates on God's law day and night.

- He will be like a tree firmly planted by streams of water.
- He yields fruit in its season.
- His leaves do not wither.
- He will prosper in all things.

This man of faith is a man who understands where he came from and where he is going. He is not one who questions God because of the events of the world. He doesn't look to the world for the answers of life. He is firmly grounded in what God assures him, even when the quakes of life occur.

In verses 4-6 we read about the faithless man:

> The wicked are not so, but they are like chaff which the wind drives away. Therefore the wicked will not stand in the judgment, nor sinners in the assembly of the righteous. For the LORD knows the way of the righteous, but the way of the wicked will perish.

Who among us would choose the end of the faithless man? Yes, men, we have two choices in how we deal with the quakes of life. Either the choice of faith or the choice of faithlessness. "As for me and my house, we will serve the LORD" (Joshua 24:15).

 Prayer

Father God, let me stand on Your promises when the quakes of life come my way, as they surely will. Give me the faith to trust Your Word. Help me lead my family into this trust. Amen.

Action

Begin today to trust God and all of His promises for you and your family. Reread Psalm 1:2-3.

Today's Wisdom

"Be still, and know that I am God."

PSALM 46:10 NIV

A good man spreads happiness
everywhere he goes, and he leaves
everyone he meets feeling a little
better than they did before. He's a
pleasure to be around, an inspiration
in good times and bad, a gift for
all seasons....He's a good man.

A good man is a gift to all who
know him—he's dependable like
the sunrise, because his goodness
springs from inner strength,
not outward circumstances.

AUTHOR UNKNOWN

We All Need Heroes

*And the angel of the L*ORD *appeared*
*to him, and said to him, "The L*ORD *is*
with you, you mighty man of valor!"

JUDGES 6:12 NKJV

To have and to hold from this day
forward, for better for worse, for richer
for poorer, in sickness and in health, to
love, honor and to cherish, until we are
parted by death. This is my solemn vow.

A MARRIAGE VOW

When a man is raising his family and praying he will have a lasting impact on his children and his grandchildren, sometimes he may wonder if the courage necessary to succeed at such a monumental job is worth it. For some men, God blesses us to see the day when we can say, "Yes, it has been worth it." One such occasion was the day I was asked to read my grandson Chad's application to the University of Oregon. Here is what he wrote:

When we think of heroes we think of people such as William Wallace, who fought for freedom, or we think of the firefighters from September 11, who died trying to save the lives of innocent men and women. The United States would not have the freedom that we have today if it wasn't for our soldiers fighting and dying for what they believed in. Those men and women are heroes as well. There are so many different types

33

of heroes, and everybody looks up to different people as their heroes. During medieval times Beowulf represented a mythical hero because of his valor, his unselfishness, and his loyalty. Today my grandfather represents a hero for his unselfishness, loyalty, and faith during times of struggle.

A hero is one who does things for others, who is loyal to his people, and who shows bravery and valor. Beowulf shows all three of these qualities throughout his story. While Beowulf's city was under attack by the dragon, he stood up, grabbed his sword, and was prepared to fight for the survival of his people and for the survival of his city. Beowulf knew that this dragon could not be defeated without the help of his sword, so he grabbed his sword and prepared to fight the dragon. Win or lose, he was prepared to fight for something—and was not fighting for himself but rather for others. This shows his loyalty to his people, his unselfishness, and his bravery and valor. He showed how brave he was when he got ready to fight something greater and bigger than him.

Heroes do not always have to win to become a hero; however, they do have to fight for something and do it with all their might and fight until they can fight no more. Beowulf proved this with his fight with the dragon, and he proved this again when he fought with Grendel. In this situation I feel that the biggest quality shown was his bravery. He fought Grendel with his bare hands, and he conquered him with no weapons other than a brave heart and desire. That is what a hero is made of, and that is what Beowulf was!

I believe that a modern-day hero should have these same qualities; however, I do not feel that the only way a man can become a hero is through fighting such as Beowulf did. I think today a man can represent a hero in many ways. I consider my grandfather one of the greatest heroes of all time. He is still alive, and he is continuing to be heroic every day he lives. My grandfather is a hero because he carries the same qualities that Beowulf carried during the medieval ages. When my grandmother was diagnosed with cancer and told that this illness would most likely take her life, our family was devastated and in tears; however, my grandfather was not. He kept faith and he kept a positive attitude. He was willing to do whatever he could to help my grandmother fight and stay alive. He showed loyalty to her and to my family by staying by her side for all the years she fought this illness. He took her to every hospital visit and stayed with her during every treatment. He kept her company and did whatever he could to keep her attitude positive.

He showed that he was unselfish by giving up his life in order to make her life last. He stopped working full-time and even sold their house in Riverside so that they could be closer to the hospital that she needed to go to. He proved that he was unselfish when he gave up hobbies that he loved in order to be with my grandma. He showed his bravery when he stayed strong even when the doctors gave him reasons not to. He was brave when they told him she was close to death and to be prepared. He was brave because he told her not to give up because he surely wasn't giving up.

My grandmother fought cancer for five years, and she has now been cancer-free for several years. My grandfather is a hero because he did not give up and he fought for my grandmother's life. She is alive today because of his heroism.

Heroes have always been and they will always be. Everybody has different heroes and every hero is a hero for their own reasons. Heroes should be thanked and heroes should be looked up to. Heroism is a quality that every human should possess and that everybody should strive to be. Because of heroes we have freedom, we have life, and we have hope—hope of success and hope of happiness. Heroes give us reason to smile and reason to rejoice. It is because of heroes that we celebrate Veterans Day and many other holidays. It is because of heroes that life is what it is.[5]

Prayer

Father God, thank You for heroes and all they do for mankind. May I be true to my marriage vow, and may I hold fast to my wife 'til death do us part. Give me the courage to be a hero to my family.

 ## Action

Be a hero to your family.

 ## Today's Wisdom

"Our trust and faithfulness produces the endurance that sees us through the 'tough stuff' we all face in this life."

ELAINE CREASMAN

A Woman's Needs

*Husbands, love your wives, just
as Christ also loved the church
and gave Himself up for her.*

EPHESIANS 5:25

After living with Emilie for more than 50 years I have been able to make several observations about what women need from us as men and husbands. I call them my "Ten Commandments of Marriage."

First Commandment—AFFECTION. Every day your wife needs many hugs to reaffirm you love her. Not only must you be a hugger, you must be a teller. You must *tell* her you love her and give her all the compliments you can think of.

Second Commandment—CONVERSATION is so very important to a woman. This is the way she gives and receives affection. Put down the paper and turn off the TV. Look her in the eye and really listen. Don't make the mistake of assuming she wants you to solve her problem. She just wants you to *listen* to the problem. She wants you to give her your undivided attention. Studies show that an average man speaks only 12,500 words per day; a woman speaks 25,000. If you have been apart during the day, your wife will have much to tell you when you're together in the evening. Listen to her.

Third Commandment—TRANSPARENCY means you are open and honest with her. You are a man of truth. Since women are more feelings-oriented than us men, they want us to share our feelings with them. When your wife senses she can trust you in who you see and what you do, she becomes very secure in the relationship. Transparency builds a great foundation for trust.

Fourth Commandment—FINANCIAL SECURITY is one of the bonding ingredients for a healthy marriage. A wife does not want to spend her time fending off creditors because of the family's money problems. Most separations and divorces are caused by money problems. Insecurity regarding finances is a burden you need not give your wife and family. You are responsible for being a good provider and for being willing to share information about your financial dealings. A wise man includes his wife in financial decisions.

Fifth Commandment—You need to be a GOOD FATHER. This role has changed dramatically in the past 30 years. Dads are expected to be more involved in parenting or raising their children than ever before. Today it's very much expected that Dad will be involved during pregnancy, present during delivery, available to change diapers—and later, be present at all school activities, recitals, and sporting events. We not only need to be good dads, but as the children get older and have their own children we are expected to be involved in the lives of our grandchildren. Research has shown that families who have involved dads have healthier family members. Many of our social problems can be related to absentee dads.

Sixth Commandment—SEXUAL FULFILLMENT is a desire of all healthy women. In the olden days we would have never listed this as a woman's need. It wasn't a topic to be discussed in public, but the twenty-first century has made us aware of this need. It's very important for us men to maintain a continuous and exciting passion for our wife. This pursuit lets her feel confident in who she is as a woman. Intimacy makes a woman's heart happy.

Seventh Commandment—COMPANIONSHIP is a strong need for a wife. In most cases they want you to be their very best friends. Men have a difficult time in relating to this because of our own concept of friendship. There are many healthy ways that we can fulfill this commandment. In general it's very important to do things together. It might be sports, going to dinner regularly, just the two of you vacationing, going to the theater, taking walks, attending church functions, and so on. Wives want togetherness—the dividends are big when we invest in spending time with our wives.

Eighth Commandment—ATTRACTIVENESS is a strong desire of our wives. They truly want us to look *sharp*. Not only do you want your wife to be attractive, she desires that you also look your best. We might feel comfortable wearing loose-fitting and casual clothes, but on occasion we need to spiff ourselves up for our wives. Check such things as your nose hair, your ear hair, and your bushy eyebrows. These must be attended to! We want our wives to be proud of our appearance. If you're not very good at determining the latest fashion, ask your wife; she will probably be more than glad to assist you in this selection process. Remember to put your best foot forward.

Ninth Commandment—DOMESTIC SUPPORT has risen its head in the last few years as a biggy on the woman's wish list. Each family has to work out its own division of labor depending on many variables within it. When more women started working out of the home, the division of labor changed. That's why there are no simple answers to this. Every couple may have a different solution. However, men can help tremendously simply by not adding to the wives' problem in taking care of the home. We need to be part of the solution and not part of the problem. Your wife is not your mother. You need to pick up your clothes, clean up after you make a mess, and assist her in training the children to take care of their personal areas. In order to have an efficient home it takes planning. Come together as a family and decide how you are going to solve this problem. It doesn't all fall on Mom's shoulders.

Tenth Commandment—ADMIRATION AND APPRECIATION is a biggy. We all want to feel worthy of what we do. Take time to express your thankfulness for all your wife does to make your home a pleasant experience. Train your children how to express their thanks for Mom's contributions. Bring home occasional flowers, a box of candy, a certificate for the spa, a pair of movie tickets, and so on. A hug and thank-you goes a long way.

 Prayer

Father God, may I become more sensitive to my wife's needs. So often I'm so concerned about my job and my desires that I don't pay enough attention to others around me. Thank You for this reminder. Amen.

 Action

ACTION

For the next ten weeks concentrate on one of these commandments for each week. Do what you can to carry out the theme. (Don't worry if your wife can't believe what she's seeing. You will certainly be more active in the sixth commandment.)

 Today's Wisdom

"The world needs fewer man-made goods and more God-made men."

SARAH ANNE JEPSON

God's Wings

*He will shield you with his
wings! They will shelter you.*

—PSALM 91:4 TLB

Not long ago I read this beautiful story, which someone wrote to illustrate God's love:

After a forest fire in Yellowstone National Park, forest rangers began their trek up a mountain to assess the inferno's damage. One ranger found a bird literally petrified in ashes, perched like a statue on the ground at the base of a tree. Somewhat sickened by the eerie sight, he knocked over the bird with a stick. Three tiny chicks scurried from under their dead mother's wings. The loving mother, keenly aware of impending disaster, had carried her offspring to the base of the tree and gathered them under her wings, instinctively knowing that the toxic smoke would rise. She could have flown to safety but had refused to abandon her babies. When the blaze had arrived and the heat had scorched her small body, the mother had remained steadfast. Because she had been willing to die, those under the cover of her wings would live.[6]

This is such a beautiful picture of what God did for us so that we might live. He sent His Son, Jesus, to the cross so that His death would atone for our sins. Just think about it—as this mother bird gave her life so her chicks might live, Jesus died so we might live. It costs us nothing, but it cost Jesus everything.

Scripture tells us husbands, "Husbands, love your wives, just as Christ also loved the church and gave Himself up for her" (Ephesians 5:25).

In America our political climate doesn't ask us to give up our lives for our wives, but in many parts of the world this is not the case. In many countries Christian men are asked to make the ultimate sacrifice for their loved ones. But that's what Jesus did for us on the cross. He was willing to die so the church might live. We are all part of the body of Christ, which makes up the church.

If, as a husband, I'm asked to be willing to die for my wife, should I not also be willing to live for her?

I continually examine my attitude toward my wife to see if my actions represent what Scripture has to say about the way I should treat my wife. Am I her leader, her protector, her provider, her security?

A pastor once asked a group of men on our retreat, "Men, is your wife a better Christian because she is married to you, or has your marriage been a hindrance to her spiritual growth?"

In small-group discussions afterward, many of the men present had to confess they were hindering the spiritual growth of their wives and children. Men, if that is our case, we must come to grips with our situation and make changes—drastic changes—in our lives. After all, we will stand before God one day and He will ask us the same question. We all will want to say we had a very positive effect on our wife's spiritual growth.

As the psalmist wrote, "I will shield you with my wings and they will shelter you" (my paraphrase). May this be our battle cry!

 Prayer

Father God, I want my "wings" to shelter my wife. May she know that I want to be her protector. Amen.

 Action

Let your wife know you love her and are her protector.

 Today's Wisdom

"Jesus obliged us to confess our sins for our own sake rather than for his…If you harm a friend, it is not enough to apologize to God—you must apologize to your friend as well."

ALFRED WILSON

Every moment we live before the face of God, and before His face there are no forgotten deeds, no disregarded words, and no inconsequential choices. Each moment is a chance to live utterly to His glory. Choose well. Live well, with wisdom and passion. Savor and show the supremacy of God in every part of your life. Place God at the center of every thought, every action, every choice, every love—at the center of all that you are and all that you do. Live passionately for Him!

JOHN PIPER

Knowing What's Important

Let not a wise man boast of his wisdom,
and let not the mighty man boast of his
might, let not a rich man boast of his riches.

JEREMIAH 9:23

Somehow I'm always curious about what's going to land in our mailbox each day. Oh, yes—we get the junk mail, the catalogs, the bills, the social-event invitations. And occasionally we get a letter that makes an impact on our life. Recently we had such a day. Buried in the midst of a large pile of envelopes and junk mail was a letter from a very special gentleman and personal friend. He happened to be a very prominent businessman in our community.

I opened the letter and began to read:

> Dear Friend and Longtime Customer,
>
> What do you do when you make a major change in your business, move and build new offices so you can be closer to your customers, and then find out that it doesn't take you back to the fun of 20 or 30 years ago in your career, and that what you are

doing now is really no longer your life goal…in fact, is really contrary to what is now important in life? I realize the only answer is to share my thoughts and ask your understanding.

I have decided to close the store and retire.

I am so very proud of our company and its position in the Inland Empire. No employer could ask for a finer bunch of people than our employees, who have given their hearts in trying to establish and maintain the professional standards we have set for ourselves and endeavored to live by. We have laughed, cried, and worked very hard together to accomplish our mission. I salute them, and thank them for allowing me to share part of my life with such a fine group as them!

This is a fast-paced and ever-changing world we live in, and retailing is no different. The furniture industry is going through a huge change on a national basis, and I am sure these changes ultimately will offer the public some new choices, which is good. As a businessperson, I must decide on the priorities, goals, and standards I am going to live and do business by, and then decide the very difficult question if I am willing to pay the price to continue a successful career.

I have never felt that I have been able to give my family the attention and energy they deserve and I desire, and I can't see that it is going to get any better…even though I always dreamed it would. The changes in retailing are most certainly not going to allow for *more* personal time! My priorities have changed. The decision was not an easy one to make, but one that will be right for me and my family.

Thank you for your attention and understanding.[7]

As I finished reading this letter, my heart was touched by its sincerity and my friend's concern for his longtime employees and customers. I had a greater concern for him and his family. Here was a man who stood tall in the saddle and was able to say that what he was doing was really no longer his life goal…in fact, it was really contrary to what was now important in life.

This is a man who has the courage to admit to himself that after 51 years of working in a family business he no longer wants to continue to sacrifice to keep it afloat.

How many of us are in the same or a similar situation? We must be willing to recognize that *goals of the past may no longer be goals of the future.*

It's okay to change direction in life. Maybe you and your wife (if you are married) need to come together and rewrite your purpose in life. After all, goals aren't carved in granite—they can be changed. We must guard our hearts to make sure we aren't caught up in the unimportant things of life. Concentrate on those things that will matter 20 years from now—your family. What good does it do a man to gain the whole world but lose his own family? With limited time here on earth we need to major on the major things of life. Break yourself away from the minor things you think are major, but really aren't.

 Prayer

Father God, let me discern what's important in my life. Make me free from spending so much energy, time, and money on things that aren't important. Amen.

Action

Be willing to rewrite some goals that need to be changed in your life. What might they be? List three. What changes will you make?

Today's Wisdom

"Clear definition of goals is the keynote of success."

EDISON MONTGOMERY

A Look at Anger

*Good sense makes a man restrain his
anger, and it is his glory to overlook
a transgression or an offense.*

PROVERBS 19:11 AMP

Anger burns like a hot brushfire. As I read my daily news-paper and view the TV news, I am constantly reminded of the sin of anger. Not a day goes by when the media doesn't report the sad results of anger: murder, road rage, drunk driving, gang warfare, arson fires, child-beating, rape, and so on.

A healthy relationship cannot exist where anger exists. The two do not go together. In order for friendships to flourish we must be able to control this raging fire that exists in most human beings. The book of Proverbs gives some insight concerning anger. These passages are all from *The Living Bible:*

- "A short-tempered man is a fool. He hates the man who is patient" (14:17).
- "A quick-tempered man starts fights; a cool-tempered man tries to stop them" (15:18).

- "It is better to be slow-tempered than famous; it is better to have self-control than to control an army" (16:32).
- "A fool gets into constant fights. His mouth is his undoing! His words endanger him" (18:6-7).
- "A short-tempered man must bear his own penalty; you can't do much to help him. If you try once you must try a dozen times!" (19:19).
- "Keep away from angry, short-tempered men, lest you learn to be like them and endanger your soul" (22:24-25).
- "A rebel shouts in anger; a wise man holds his temper in and cools it" (29:11).
- "There is more hope for a fool than for a man of quick temper" (29:20).
- "A hot-tempered man starts fights and gets into all kinds of trouble" (29:22).

If anger is one of your enemies, go to God in prayer and ask for healing. Anger is a cancer that can destroy your body if not addressed. Don't wait until it's too late. Healthy relationships demand that anger be conquered.[8]

 Prayer

Father God, help me examine myself to see if there is any evidence of anger. If so, I want to give it to You. May You help me conquer this dragon that wants to destroy me. Amen.

Action

Examine yourself to see if there is any anger in your soul.

Today's Wisdom

"All anger is not sinful, because some degree of it, and on some occasions, is inevitable. But it becomes sinful and contradicts the rule of Scripture when it is conceived upon slight and inadequate provocation, and when it continues long."

WILLIAM PALEY

If My People Pray

*If My people who are called by My
name humble themselves and pray, and
seek My face and turn from their wicked
ways, then I will hear from heaven, will
forgive their sin, and will heal their land.*

2 CHRONICLES 7:14

A poor Macedonian soldier marching ahead of Alexander the Great was leading a mule laden with gold for the king's use. The mule became so tired it could no longer carry the load, so the mule driver took it off and carried it himself, with great difficulty, for a considerable distance. Finally Alexander saw him sinking under the burden and about to throw it to the ground, so he cried out, "Friend, do not be weary yet; try to carry it to your tent, for it is now all yours."

This blessing is much better than the lottery. Who says, "Good guys finish last"? Humility certainly has its blessings. Ezra, the writer of 1 and 2 Chronicles, certainly knew the importance of humility, because he directed the above verse of Scripture to his people, people who God called by name. He states that in order for God's people to receive His blessings, there are four basic requirements:

- humility
- prayer
- devotion
- repentance

This is an appropriate prayer for all of America. We shake our heads with disbelief at the depravity of man. Each day the headlines in the media scream out stabbings, shootings, murder, rape, wars, drunkenness, and incest. Where have we gone wrong as a nation? Are we losing those qualities that have made America strong? Are our families breaking apart along with the moral fiber of this country? How can we get back on track?

Ezra says we are to humble ourselves, pray, seek God's face, and repent of our sins. God will

- answer our prayers
- forgive our sins
- heal our land

As the spiritual leader of your home, may you recognize the truths of this passage and come to God with all humility, committing your life again to the righteousness of God.

Make a vow that in your home you will make a difference. No longer will you go along with the tide of the country. You and your family will say, "Stop! No more! Let's return to the timeless principles written in the Bible."

Today, we need families who will not only believe the Bible but who will begin to live it in their daily lives.

Prayer

Father God, let this humility begin with my family. As husband and father, give me the courage to make a difference. May each member of our family be excited about this new beginning. Amen.

Action

Read this verse at dinner tonight and see what discussion comes from your family.

Today's Wisdom

"Pride changed angels into devils; humility makes men into angels."

AUGUSTINE OF HIPPO

The Trouble Tree

Even if you should suffer for the
sake of righteousness you are blessed.
And do not fear their intimidation
and do not be troubled.

1 PETER 3:14

ere's a great story about what to do with your problems:

I hired a plumber to help me restore an old farmhouse. His first day on the job was rough: A flat tire made him lose an hour of work, his electric drill quit, and his ancient one-ton truck refused to start.

While I drove him home, he sat in stony silence. On arriving he invited me in to meet his family. As we walked toward the front door, he paused briefly at a small tree, touching the tips of the branches with both hands.

Opening the door, he underwent an amazing transformation. His tanned face was wreathed in smiles, and he hugged his two small children and gave his wife a kiss.

Afterward he walked me to the car. We passed the tree, and my curiosity got the better of me. I asked him about what I had seen him do earlier.

"Oh, that's my trouble tree," he replied. "I know I can't help having troubles on the job, but one thing's for sure, those troubles don't belong in the house with my wife and the children. So I just hang them up on the tree every night when I come home and ask God to take care of them. Then in the morning I pick them up again.

"Funny thing is," he smiled, "when I come out in the morning to pick them up, there aren't nearly as many as I remember hanging up the night before."[9]

Prayer

Father God, help me not to be troubled. Help me put all of my problems at the foot of the cross. I don't want my troubles to interfere with my family. Let me relax in Your provisions. Amen.

Action

Choose one of your trees to become your trouble tree. If no trees are available, *plant one.*

Today's Wisdom

"It is distrust of God to be troubled about what is to come; impatience against God to be troubled with what is present; and anger at God to be troubled for what is past."

SIMON PATRICK

"I've Sacrificed My Son for You"

You know that it was not with perishable things such as silver or gold that you were redeemed...but with the precious blood of Christ.

1 PETER 1:18-19 NIV

After you read the following allegory, you'll think differently about the sacrifice God made for you by letting His Son die for your sins.

The time was the Roaring Twenties. The place was Oklahoma. John Griffith was in his early 20s—newly married and full of optimism. Along with his lovely wife, he had been blessed with a beautiful, blue-eyed baby. With delight and excitement, John was dreaming the American dream.

He wanted to be a traveler. He imagined what it would be like to visit faraway places with strange-sounding names. He would read about them and research them. His hopes and dreams were so vivid that at times they seemed more real than reality itself. But then came 1929 and the great stock-market crash.

With the shattering of the American economy came the devastation of John's dreams. The winds that howled through Oklahoma were strangely symbolic of the gale force that was sweeping away his hopes. Oklahoma was being systematically ravaged by depression and despair.

And so, brokenhearted, John packed up his few possessions and with his wife and little son, Greg, headed east in an old Model-A Ford. They made their way toward Missouri, to the edge of the Mississippi, and there he found a job tending one of the great railroad bridges that spanned the massive river.

Day after day John would sit in the control room and direct the enormous gears of an immense bridge over the mighty river. He would look out wistfully as bulky barges and splendid ships glided gracefully under his elevated bridge. Then, mechanically, he would lower the massive structure and stare pensively into the distance as great trains roared by and became little more than specks on the horizon. Each day he looked on sadly as they carried with them his shattered dreams and his visions of far-off places and exotic destinations.

It wasn't until 1937 that a new dream began to be born in his heart. His young son was now eight years old, and John had begun to catch a vision for a new life, a life in which Greg would work shoulder-to-shoulder with him, a life of intimate fellowship and friendship. The first day of this new life dawned and brought with it new hope and a fresh purpose. Excitedly they packed their lunches and, arm in arm, headed off toward the immense bridge.

Greg looked on in wide-eyed amazement as his dad pressed down the huge lever that raised and lowered the vast bridge. As he watched, he thought his father must surely be the greatest man alive. He marveled that his dad could single-handedly control the movements of such a stupendous structure.

Before they knew it, noontime had arrived. John had just elevated the bridge and allowed some scheduled ships to pass through. And then, taking his son by the hand, he headed off for lunch. Hand in hand, the two inched their way down a narrow catwalk and out onto an observation deck that projected some 50 feet over the majestic Mississippi. There they sat and watched spellbound as the ships passed by below.

As they ate, John told his son, in vivid detail, stories about the marvelous destinations of the ships that glided below them. Enveloped in a world of thought, he related story after story, his son hanging on every word.

Then, suddenly, in the midst of telling a tale about the time the river had overflowed its banks, he and his son were startled back to reality by the shrieking whistle of a distant train. Looking at his watch in disbelief, John saw this it was already 1:07. Immediately he remembered that the bridge was still raised and that the Memphis Express would be by in just minutes.

Not wanting to alarm his son, he suppressed his panic. In the calmest tone he could muster, he instructed his son to stay put. Quickly leaping to his feet, he jumped onto the catwalk. As the precious seconds flew by, he ran at full tilt to the steel ladder leading into the control house.

Once in, he searched the river to make sure that no ships were in sight. And then, as he had been trained to do, he looked straight down beneath the bridge to make certain nothing was below. As his eyes moved downward, he saw something so horrifying that his heart froze in his chest. For there below him, in the massive gearbox that housed the colossal gears that moved the gigantic bridge, was his beloved son.

Apparently Greg had tried to follow his dad but had fallen off the catwalk. Even now he was wedged between the teeth of two main cogs in the gearbox. Although he appeared to be conscious, John could see that his son's leg had already begun to bleed profusely. Immediately an even more horrifying thought flashed through his mind. For in that instant he knew that lowering the bridge meant killing the apple of his eye.

Panicked, his mind probed in every direction, frantically searching for solutions. Suddenly a plan emerged. In his mind's eye he saw himself grabbing a coiled rope, climbing down the ladder, running toward the catwalk, securing the rope, sliding down toward his son, and pulling him back up to safety. Then in an instant he would move back down toward the control lever and thrust it down just in time for the oncoming train.

As soon as these thoughts appeared, he realized the futility of his plan. Instantly, he knew that there just wouldn't be enough time. Perspiration began to bead on John's brow, terror written over every inch of his face. His mind darted here and there, vainly searching for yet another solution. What would he do? What could he do?

His thoughts rushed in anguish to the oncoming train. In a state of panic, his agonized mind considered the 400 people that were moving inexorably closer toward the bridge. Soon the train would come roaring out of the trees with tremendous speed. But this—this was his son...his only child...his pride...his joy.

His mother—he could see her tear-stained face now. This was their child, their beloved son. He was his father and this was his boy.

He knew in a moment there was only one thing he could do. He knew he would have to do it. And so, burying his face under his left arm, he plunged down the lever. The cries of his son were quickly drowned out by the sound of the bridge as it ground slowly into position. With only seconds to spare, the Memphis Express—with its 400 passengers—roared out of the trees and across the mighty bridge.

John Griffith lifted his tear-streaked face and looked into the windows of the passing train. A businessman was reading the morning newspaper. A uniformed conductor was glancing nonchalantly at his large vest pocket watch. Ladies were already sipping their afternoon tea in the dining cars. A small boy, looking strangely like his own son, Greg, pushed a long thin spoon into a large dish of ice cream. Many of the passengers seemed to be engaged in either idle conversation or careless laughter.

But no one looked his way. No one even cast a glance at the giant gearbox that housed the mangled remains of his hopes and dreams.

In anguish he pounded the glass in the control room and cried out, "What's the matter with you people? Don't you care? Don't you know I've sacrificed my son for you? What's wrong with you?"

No one answered; no one heard. No one even looked. Not one of them seemed to care. And then, as suddenly as it had happened, it was over. The train disappeared, moving rapidly across the bridge and out over the horizon.[10]

Even now as I retell this story, my face is wet with tears. For this illustration is but a faint glimpse of what God the Father did for us in sacrificing His Son, Jesus, to atone for the sins of the world (John 3:16). However, unlike the Memphis Express that caught John Griffith by surprise, God—in His great love and according to His sovereign will and purpose—determined to sacrifice His Son so we might live (1 Peter 1:19-20). Not only that, but the consummate love of Christ is demonstrated in that He was not accidentally "caught," as was John Griffith's son. Rather, He willingly sacrificed His life for the sins of mankind (John 10:18; see also Matthew 26:53).

 ### Prayer

Father God, my heart aches as I read today's devotion. It's hard for me to imagine having to make that kind of decision. In a very small way I get a sense of what You, our heavenly Father, had to go through when You sent Your Son to earth to die for our sins. I thank You for making that kind of sacrifice. You are truly a God of endless love. Amen.

Action

Spend some time in prayer thanking God for making the ultimate sacrifice of His only Son for our sins.

Today's Wisdom

"Was anything real ever gained without sacrifice of some kind?"

ARTHUR HELPS

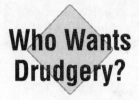

Who Wants Drudgery?

*In everything [we commend] ourselves as
servants of God, in much endurance, in
afflictions, in hardships, in distresses, in
beatings, in imprisonments, in tumults,
in labors, in sleeplessness, in hunger...*

2 CORINTHIANS 6:4-5

Has anyone ever said, "I love drudgery"? I sincerely doubt it.

I know I wake up each day hoping I don't have to endure drudgery today—particularly in the area of relationships. Wouldn't it be great if, as husband and wife, there were no problems and we only had to do things that were fun? Our society says, "Only do it if it feels good." Yet, if we did only the feel-good things, we would never have the opportunity to experience those things that develop true Christian character.

Author Charles Kingsley wisely said,

> Thank God every morning when you get up that
> you have something to do which must be done,
> whether you like it or not. Being forced to work,
> and forced to do your best, will breed in you temperance and self-control, diligence and strength of

will, cheerfulness and content, and a hundred virtues which the idle never know.

If we rise up and let our lives shine during the doing of tasks that are drudgery, we can witness transfiguration that makes drudgery divine.

How do we transform the mundane into the divine? Our Scripture for today says that as a servant of God we commend ourselves in every way in

- great endurance
- troubles
- hardship
- hunger
- purity
- understanding
- and other things

Paul, who wrote these words, knew how to take the drudgeries of life and turn them into something divine. In today's language, he knew how to turn lemons into lemonade.

How can we take all of our drudgeries and make them divine? Only when we become servants to each other and let the Holy Spirit strengthen us beyond our human efforts.

Oswald Chambers says,

> Drudgery is one of the finest touchstones of character there is. Drudgery is work that is very far removed from anything to do with the ideal—the utterly mean, grubby things; and when we come in contact with them we know instantly whether or not we are spiritually real.[11]

Drudgery must have the inspiration of God in order for us to see it in His proper light. Christ's death on the cross was certainly the greatest form of drudgery, but it was vitally necessary for our salvation. None of our drudgeries will ever be that demanding.

Prayer

Father God, as we look upon the everyday drudgeries of life may we recognize our servanthood to You. May we see the eternal light in these tasks, so we can recognize You are building eternal character in our lives. Amen.

Action

Examine two or three of your drudgeries to see how God can make these into virtues.

Today's Wisdom

When things go wrong, as they sometimes will,
When the road you're trudging seems all uphill,
When the funds are low and the debts are high,
And you want to smile, but you have to sigh,
When care is pressing you down a bit,
Rest, if you must—but don't quit.

Life is queer with its twists and turns,
As every one of us sometimes learns,
And many a failure turns about
When he might have won had he stuck it out;
Don't give up, though the pace seems slow—
You might succeed with another blow.

Often the goal is nearer than
It seems to a faint and faltering man,
Often the struggler has given up

When he might have captured the victor's cup.
And he learned too late, when the night slipped down,
How close he was to the golden crown.

Success is failure turned inside out—
The silver tint of the clouds of doubt—
And you never can tell how close you are,
It may be near when it seems afar;
So stick to the fight when you're hardest hit—
It's when things seem worst that you must not quit.[12]

Honesty—Living
with Integrity

*Lying lips are an abomination
to the LORD, but those who deal
faithfully are His delight.*

PROVERBS 12:22

One of the rapidly disappearing character traits in America is honesty among men. Every day there are headlines that expose the dishonesty of prominent personalities in sports, business, church, and politics. Men seem to have a difficult time in not crossing the line that separates honest behavior from dishonest behavior.

Somehow we don't want to fudge much—just do a little bending of the law. Brothers, when we think in that fashion we are heading for trouble. Most of us don't wake up each morning and say, "Today I'm going to be dishonest." Instead, we bend a little here and bend a little there; over a period of time we are willing to bend more and more, and eventually those bends are no longer so little. These small bends grow into bigger bends, and one day we become a man who has lost honesty as a part of his character.

In life, I find there are three areas where I must be honest.

Area 1: I will be honest with myself in...

- what I think (Proverbs 4:23)
- what I say (Proverbs 4:24)
- what I see (Proverbs 4:25)
- where I walk (Proverbs 4:26)
- what I do (Proverbs 4:27)

Area 2: I will be honest with others and...

- speak the truth (Proverbs 12:17)
- speak the truth in love (Ephesians 4:15)
- speak the truth in love with tact (Proverbs 15:23)

Area 3: I will be honest with God because...

- the truth is in His Word (John 8:31)
- the truth sets us free (John 8:32)
- trusting the truth brings freedom unlike any other (John 8:36)

If we can be honest with ourselves, with others, and with God, we are equipped to go out into the world and live victoriously. We can play the game by the rules, and we can be at peace with ourselves, with others, and with God. We will be set free to become the man God envisioned when we were in our mother's womb.

Each day we're challenged to be men of honor. Each day we must choose to abide by the rules of man and the rules of God. When we do, we are set free to be honest men.

Prayer

Father God, I want to be a man who has integrity, one who has honor, and one who has become a free man. Give me the strength each day to be an honest man. I appreciate Your standing beside me today and every day. Amen.

 Action

Evaluate your life today. Are there areas that need to be adjusted? If so, what are you going to change so you experience the freedom Christ can bring?

 Today's Wisdom

"I hope I shall possess firmness and virtue enough to maintain what I consider the most enviable of all titles, the character of an honest man."

GEORGE WASHINGTON

Making Strong Families

*That man will never be unwelcome
to others who makes himself
agreeable to his own family.*

PLAUTUS

One of the joys of life is being part of a well-functioning family. One of my reasons for getting married at the relatively young age of 22 was to be a husband first and a father second.

Back then, we didn't have all the self-help books and seminars we do today. All I knew was that I had a healthy mom and dad and two wonderful brothers. With those models I naturally wanted to duplicate the same family unit. Being raised in a Christian church I had been taught that God had ordained marriage (Genesis 2:24; Mark 10:9; 1 Corinthians 11:11; 1 Timothy 3:2; and Hebrews 13:4), and I was ready to leave my parents and cleave to my wife.

I wasn't sure what it took to make a healthy family. All I saw was that my mom and dad loved each other and they loved us boys. Since those early days, much research has been done in the study of what components help to make healthy families.

Even though we didn't know about these components as such, we can look back to our family and say, Yes, I agree—we had these elements; and yes, they contributed to our success.

What are a few of these components?

- commitment to the family unit
- ability to express affection and appreciation
- keeping conversation positive
- spending valuable time together
- encouraging spiritual faith
- being able to deal healthily with conflict

Commitment to the family unit. Be committed to the marriage and family unit. Healthy families know each individual is committed to each other and to family unity. Divorce was never an option for us. It wasn't even in our vocabulary. Our theme verse was Mark 10:9: "What...God has joined together, let no man separate."

The family always comes first. This is sometimes difficult during the teenage years, but we stressed the importance of sticking together, particularly around birthdays, holidays, Sunday church, anniversaries, and other special occasions. In order for us to have time to do this, we had to reduce the number of outside activities we each had. These together times went on our family calendar, thus letting all members know this was important to us all.

We all pitched in to do the chores—yes, even Mom and Dad. Our home was something that belonged to us all. Our family made a big deal over special occasions. These traditions built in a lot of togetherness. Even today, though our children are grown and there are five grandchildren, we still celebrate these special events.

To this day, if Mom and Dad don't call on the telephone

early on the mornings of our kids' birthdays to sing "Happy Birthday," they are so disappointed.

Another way to solidify commitment to family is to build an awareness of our history. We have photographs framed of important family members throughout our home. Even though my dad has been gone for more than 30 years, and even though the grandchildren never met him, they know all about Papa J.K. We show them his pictures and tell stories about what kind of man he was.

On each of the children's and grandchildren's birthdays we take out their individual photo albums and let them thumb through to see the early years of their lives. They look forward to this time together so much.

Another way to encourage family commitment is to have, at least once a month, a meeting for the whole family to discuss any areas of concern. There are no topics taboo. This gives each family member an opportunity to review rules that need to be evaluated, or mention other adjustments to family life that need to be considered. We did this often on Friday night at the local hamburger joint before a high-school sporting event.

Ability to express affection and appreciation. There was a mom who found her young son out in the barn in a room full of horse manure, digging like mad. She asked her boy, "What are you doing digging through all this manure?" The son replied, "Mom, with all this manure there's got to be a pony here someplace." Here was a young man whose glass was half full. That quality comes from the times when we build up and encourage our family members. We tell the positive. We all want to be appreciated. My family, while I was growing up, were huggers and kissers. So when I grew up that's what I thought a person should do. We need to be appreciative of each other, and our children will follow suit. We hug, kiss, and say, "I love you," every day. One of our favorite stickers is a teddy bear with the words "I was caught being good" on the front. When someone was caught being good we would make a big deal out of it and stick one on their shirt or blouse. They wore it with pride.

Another tool that our family used was sharing the "Red Plate." It is a regular-size plate that has these words printed in white around the border: "You Are Special Today." This plate is given on special occasions when a member of the family is worthy of praise—birthdays, graduation, making the honor roll, good grades, and so on. After the meal, we go around the table and reaffirm why the person is special. These are great mealtimes.

Keeping conversation positive. Our theme verse that kept our family on focus on this valuable trait is found in Ephesians 4:29:

> Let no unwholesome word proceed from your mouth, but only such a word as is good for edification according to the need of the moment, that it may give grace to those who hear.

People will feel more respected and encouraged when conversation is positive. Our family was never permitted to be caustic and negative to each other. That language was not acceptable. Our present-day TV sitcoms are filled with family members using caustic language with one another. No wonder we have such cynical language in our society. Words most children hear are negative. It's so important to be courteous when someone is speaking. We encourage courtesy in conversing together. As a father I demanded the children speak respectfully to their mom—if not because of her mom status, most assuredly because she was my wife. Do you know what happened? They have always been respectful of both Mom and Dad.

Spending valuable time together. One of the surest ways to build family identity is by spending time together. We live in a merry-go-round world. Each year we go faster and faster. As dads we have to make time for family togetherness. There has been a revitalized priority for dinner (supper if you are in the South) together. Schedule an appropriate time when all family members can attend.

One of our traditions was to go to a local coffee shop on Sunday mornings before church and have breakfast. Mom just loved this idea because it relieved her of preparing breakfast while making sure everyone was ready for church.

When the children were in junior-high school we had a pool and spa. A heated spa with popcorn, soft drinks, and a lot of laughs were great glue to hold our family together.

Other ideas? Rent a movie and have a "do nothing" evening. Get in your pajamas and slippers, climb up on the sofa, and just do nothing but hang out. These are the times when conversation is at its best.

I, as "PaPa Bob," have a "PaPa Bob Adventure" with the grandchildren. They never know what I'm going to plan, but they always know it's going to be a lot of fun. They don't dare not go, because they know it's going to be good. It's usually a simple thing like getting an ice-cream cone or visiting a nearby zoo, but they're always up for the adventure. Make not only quality but also quantity time to build togetherness.

Encouraging spiritual faith. You can only pass on what's important to you. For me it was easy to pass along my faith. For our family it was already part of our routine. Church-related activities have played such a large part in making our family who we are. Sunday school, summer and winter camps, mission trips, feeding the homeless—these all have been contributors to what's spiritually important to the adults as well as children and now grandchildren.

Our devotional times around the table helped us to be able to talk about the big issues of life. We were able to talk about eternal values, not just short-term values. These values have been transmitted into our kids' adult life and are now being recreated in their families.

Being able to deal healthily with conflict. Learning how to deal with conflict is one of the most valuable lessons in life. Crises cause the strong to unite and become stronger. If our families exhibit a wholesome attitude with the previous five elements of a healthy family, this one will be much easier to teach.

When in conflict, we tried to teach that conflict isn't personal. Often during the heat of the disagreement, we have to have time out before we are able to discuss the disagreement. Try to buy time. It's not always necessary to resolve the conflict at that specific time. Discuss it when everyone has control of their emotions.

A lot of time family members get on edge when they are tired and lack good, healthy activities. During any conflict resolution we must remain courteous. We need to teach how to fight and disagree fairly.

 Prayer

Father God, my heart's desire is to have a strong, healthy family. Help me to evaluate my family and transmit to our family members how to relate better one to another. Give me the wisdom to follow through on my desire. Amen.

 Action

Take one of these areas each week (for six weeks) and evaluate, redirect, and motivate change where you see a deficiency. Bring these observations to your family and discuss. As a family, plan on ways to improve in each area.

 Today's Wisdom

"Our house ought to be a little church, with 'Holiness to the Lord' over the door; but it ought never to be a prison, where there is plenty of rule and order, but little love and no pleasure. Married life is not all sugar, but grace in the heart will keep away most of the sours."

C.H. SPURGEON

"Walk a little slower, Daddy,"
said a little child so small.

"I'm following in your footsteps
and I don't want to fall.

"Sometimes your steps are very fast,
sometimes they're hard to see;

"So, walk a little slower, Daddy,
for you are leading me.

"Someday when I'm all grown
up, you're what I want to be.

"Then I will have a little child
who'll want to follow me.

"And I would want to lead just
right, and know that I was true;

"So, walk a little slower, Daddy,
for I must follow you!"

AUTHOR UNKNOWN

The Legacy of Being a Father

Honor your father and your mother,
that your days may be prolonged.

EXODUS 20:12

A couple of years ago I received the best letter a father could ever receive. My daughter took the time to honor me with a letter of her thoughts about me. As I read this letter my heart was touched by her sweet, tender, and sincere words. Tears came to my eyes as each sentence was relived in my mind. After reading her comments I thought to myself, *Thank You, Lord, for showing me how to be a godly man!* Without a doubt my life has left a legacy for my daughter.

Dear Dad, on Father's Day:

Let's just start out by saying I am very grateful to have you as my father.

Thank you, Dad, for just being you.

Thank you, Dad, for being there when I was a little girl. You gave me such a feeling of family and most of all "LOVE." Also a lot of support in the areas I needed. As I grew older you still were there for me but in a different way. You still gave me family, love, and support, but you also taught me how to be a young lady, and on my sixteenth birthday, about the birds and the bees.

Thank you for your time you gave me during those teenage years. In high school at Poly, I will never forget you and Mom always at the football games watching Brad play and me being the freckle-faced varsity cheerleader. Boy, were those great times for our family. I thank you for the Friday nights at Coco's for dinner. Then after dinner you always said, "Okay, you and Brad can now go do your thing with your friends. Be careful, and I love you."

Thank you for making church on Sunday a must and keeping the Barnes family together. At times I know it must have been hard, Dad, but you were strong and had an awesome commitment to God. Thank you for showing me God's way, so when I die one day, I will go to heaven. You told me about God. I am truly blessed.

Thank you, Dad, for accepting me even when I was losing or making mistakes and errors in judgment, or when I couldn't promise you I was giving my best.

Thank you, Dad, for loving my three children and always being there for them at all times. The pool birthday parties on Rumsey are great memories for the kids. You were always so giving of your Barn for the kids. Everyone always had so much fun swimming, eating, playing, and having birthday cake. You, Dad, always made the parties a lot of fun and were there to help clean up and water down the driveway.

As time goes on, we all start growing up. Kids get bigger and bigger, sports, church activities, plays, and so on...Dad, you've been there to support the family in all those areas, and I want to thank you. During those tough times you always stood firm on your beliefs and spoke only the truth—what Scripture would say to us. You always encouraged me to listen to others, reach out to people, and listen to what God was telling me (thank you). At times I know it was hard to believe in me, but you did. I knew I would come through this rocky road and see the light one day. It all took time and a lot of prayer. Thank you for always praying for me, Dad! Time goes on, and life is good for all of us.

Dad, I want to honor you on this special day for the man I saw when my mom had cancer. You turned my world around watching. You took care of our sick mom. What a man you are!

Dad, I saw a side of you I've never seen before. You became such a wonderful caregiver to Mom. Growing up, Mom cooked, cleaned, and did all the motherly chores—and Dad, you would sit in your green-leather chair after a hard day at work and read your newspaper and relax, not a care in the world. But things changed really fast. I saw Mom in the green-leather chair and my dad cooking, cleaning, and doing *all* the motherly chores. Thank you for being there for Mom during those hard, scary days. But you always had a smile and trusted in God that everything would be fine one day. I trusted in your words. You always read the Bible to Mom and prayed over her. I saw all this during the sick days at "Sea Island."

Boy, did our lives change! But through it all we all became so much closer as a family. At least I saw life a lot differently and saw God with different eyes. For the first time I really started believing in the power of prayer. I began to pray every day for my sick mom too. Looking back to the time I was a little girl, I see God did have a plan for our family, but I never thought it would be my mom having cancer.

Dad, you are an amazing man, and I want to honor you on this Father's Day! I've never met a man at all like you. You are a true blessing from God. Your obedience to God has surely shown me a lot as well as thousands of people in our world. We need more men like you.

Time goes on, and here we are in 2002. What a gift from God Mom is to all of us—healed, and now you and Mom can start over with a new life together. Dad, you have never given up HOPE! Thank you for showing me the right road in life, and that was *God!*

I could write forever, Dad, but I hope you can feel my feelings toward you. I can't express my feelings enough to you, but I hope this letter helps. I've never been very good at writing my feelings. But I really wanted to share with you a little bit of my heart on this special day. My Bill—he is a great man, Dad, and in so many ways he reminds me of you. And I love it. I feel God brought Bill into my life to be my husband for two reasons—he loves our family, and it's exciting to see how God works in our lives.

I am proud and honored to call you my DAD—the best man I know, the one who has given my life hope and a true family.

Thank you for everything—especially for being yourself and loving Mom. Have a great day. You're the best-ever Dad!

I love you!
Jenny[13]

Like most men, I've wondered if my life has made an impact on those people most important to me. A letter like this is such a wonderful affirmation that my attempts to be a good husband and father have made a difference. It also reinforces my belief that children learn more by example than by lectures.

I'm humbled and blessed I've had such a positive influence on my daughter. I pray every father could and would live a life to receive such a letter from his child. Who you are as a father *now* will determine your legacy as a dad. May you be as blessed as I have been.

Prayer

Father God, may I be the kind of husband, father, and man *now* that will result in a legacy for those closest to me in future years. Thank You for being a model Father for me. Amen.

 Action

Go out and create your legacy for your children.

 Today's Wisdom

"A good leader takes a little more than his share of blame; a little less than his share of credit."

ARNOLD H. GLASGOW

What Is Success?

A few summers ago our family rented a modest cabin at Lake Arrowhead in the San Bernardino mountains of Southern California about two hours from our home. It was going to be a quiet getaway to read, rest, and relax. We don't get to do these three R's enough.

During the course of the three days up there, my attention was drawn to an old dusty framed piece that hung in one of the bathrooms. As I took time to read it I found this collection of thoughts on success:

> Great people are just ordinary people with an extraordinary amount of determination.
>
> There is no gain without pain.
>
> When you fail to plan, you plan to fail.
>
> Change your thoughts and you can change your world.

There are infinite possibilities in little beginnings if God is in them.

Build a dream and the dream will build you.

Inch by inch, anything is a cinch.

Don't let impossibilities intimidate you, do let possibilities motivate you.

Make your decisions on "God's ability," not your ability.

What you are is God's gift to you; what you make of yourself is your gift to God.

It's possible to face the music with God's Son in your heart.

God's delays are not God's denials.

I'd rather attempt to do something great and fail than attempt to do nothing and succeed.

Look at what you have left, not at what you have lost.

Find a hurt and heal it.

You are God's project and God never fails.

As I finished reading this I began to think upon this concept of success. Today our media tries to bombard us with all the materialism of the universe to make us compare our own adventure with all that the world has to offer. My first thoughts were that if material success brought happiness then all the wealthy people of the world would be very happy and all the poor people would be very sad—but that's really the opposite of what I've observed.

Then I asked myself, *What is success?* A quote from the past flashed through my brain: *Success is progressive realization of worthwhile goals!* Yes, that's the whole idea of success.

That must mean my wife and I have to sit down and think through some worthwhile goals and then attain them over a period of time. They aren't instantly attainable; they are progressively realized—postponed gratifications, if you will.

Two common barriers that prevent most people from reaching their goals are...

1. We have made a habit of past failures and mistakes.

2. We fear failure.

Because of these two negatives, many of us never reach our potential.

As you think through today's thoughts you may want to do some homework on your definition of success. (A good reference for establishing proper priorities and goal setting is found in my wife Emilie's book *More Hours in My Day*. See especially chapters 4, 7, 9, and 10.)[14]

 Prayer

> Father God, help me clearly think through this whole concept of what makes for success. The world gives one definition that is short-lived, but I elect to go the eternal way. Protect my heart as I think this through. Amen.

 Action

> Sit down with your spouse and write some goals for your lives.

 Today's Wisdom

> "Never undertake anything for which you wouldn't have the courage to ask the blessings of heaven."
>
> G.C. LICHTENBERG

God wishes to dwell in us in poverty
without any of the trappings for
which we win so much praise. All he
wishes to be is the sole object and
only enchantment of our hearts.

JEAN-PIERRE DE CAUSSADE,
The Sacrament of the Present Moment

Words of Silver and Gold

*The Lord's promise is sure. He speaks
no careless word; all he says is purest
truth, like silver seven times refined.*

PSALM 12:6 TLB

The common language today has taken a turn for the worse. As each decade passes, it seems the quality of words and thought has gone downhill. Just go to the mall, or listen to the words of others in the next booth at the restaurant or even the words on nightly television…and you can't believe what you hear. Not only are they vulgar, they are not clear in thought.

Words carry a lot of power. We need to be very careful in the words we choose in communicating with others. Often there is a lot of unintentional humor in speech that's not clearly thought through.

For example, here are some rib-tickling excerpts from insurance claim forms.[15] In each case, the insured was asked to succinctly state what had caused an automobile accident:

- "The other car collided with mine without warning me of its intentions."

- "I had been shopping for plants all day and was on my way home. As I reached an intersection, a hedge sprang up obscuring my vision. I did not see the other car."

- "I had been driving my car for 40 years when I fell asleep at the wheel and had the accident."

- "I pulled away from the side of the road, glanced at my mother-in-law, and headed over the embankment."

- "The pedestrian had no idea which direction to go, so I ran over him."

- "I told the police that I was not injured; but upon removing my hat, I found that I had fractured my skull."

- "I was unable to stop in time and my car crashed into the other vehicle. The driver and passenger left immediately for a vacation with injuries."

- "An invisible car came out of nowhere, struck my car, and vanished."

- "The indirect cause of this accident was a little guy, in a small car, with a big mouth."

- "A truck backed into my wife's face."

- "The guy was all over the road. I swerved many times before I hit him."

- "I collided with a stationary truck coming the other way. To avoid hitting the bumper of the car in front, I struck the pedestrian."

- "As I approached the intersection, a stop sign suddenly appeared in a place where no stop sign had ever appeared before."

- "The telephone pole was approaching fast. I was attempting to swerve out of its path when it struck my front end."

 ## Prayer

Father, let me have a good way with words. May they ring like silver and gold. May I be very careful in the words I utter. May they be pleasing to the ear of the hearer. Amen.

 ## Action

Evaluate your speech to see how it measures up to wholesomeness.

 ## Today's Wisdom

A godly man sets a new standard for doing business as well as for being married and fathering.

Put On the New

*Choose life in order that you may
live, you and your descendants.*

DEUTERONOMY 30:19

L ife is a strange journey. We have two choices to make. We
choose either life or death. It's that basic. Not too much
mental power is needed to figure this formula out.

> If any man is in Christ, he is a new creature; the old
> things passed away; behold new things have come
> (2 Corinthians 5:17).

What are these old things? They are the natural things that
men are born with. The man with all his sinful nature. Those
things that we need to flee from. Colossians 3:5-9 reads,

> Put to death the sinful, earthly things lurking within
> you. Have nothing to do with sexual sin, impurity,
> lust, and shameful desires. Don't be greedy for the
> good things of this life, for that is idolatry. God's
> terrible anger will come upon those who do such
> things. You used to do them when your life was

still part of this world. But now is the time to get rid of anger, rage, malicious behavior, slander, and dirty language. Don't lie to each other, for you have stripped off your evil nature and all its wicked deeds (NLT).

These are the things we need to put off:

- anger
- rage
- malicious behavior
- slander
- dirty language
- lying

You might ask, "Boy, do I have to give up all of these? What harm is there in keeping a few?" When you choose to keep any one of these, in essence you are choosing death. We must come clean and realize that these will eventually pull us away from God. He has a plan that spells out life, and His perfect will for our lives is that we run as fast as we can from these death items. It means we will be choosing new friends, telling different jokes, reading different magazines, holding our tongue when we want to scream in anger. No more gossiping or drinking with the boys until late in the evening. These are all death angels to relationships and particularly our marriage and family.

If not these, what must I put on? What does the new life look like?

In its place you have clothed yourselves with a brand-new nature that is continually being renewed as you learn more and more about Christ, who created this new nature within you. In this new life, it doesn't matter if you are Jew or Gentile, circumcised or uncircumcised, barbaric, uncivilized, slave or free.

Christ is all that matters, and he lives in all of us. Since God chose you to be holy people whom he loves, you must clothe yourselves with tenderhearted mercy, kindness, humility, gentleness and patience. You must make allowance for each other's faults and forgive the person who offends you. Remember, the Lord forgave you, so you must forgive others. And the most important piece of clothing you must wear is love (Colossians 3:10-14 NLT).

What do we need to put on?

- mercy
- kindness
- humility
- gentleness
- patience
- forgiveness
- love

We must be willing to take those things off that lead to death and to put on those things that give life.

 Prayer

Father God, give me the courage and strength to take off those things that will prevent me from being all You want me to be. I so want to be a man after Your own heart. Amen.

Action

Make a list of the things you want to put off. Save some room to list what you're going to do to put them off. Give yourself a deadline for accomplishing each. Then do the same for what you want to put on.

Today's Wisdom

"The fruit of the Spirit is love, joy, peace, patience, kindness, goodness, faithfulness, gentleness, self-control; against such things there is no law."

GALATIANS 5:22-23

Be Thankful and Content in All Things

*Bless the L*ORD, *O my soul; and all
that is within me, bless His holy
name. Bless the L*ORD, *O my soul,
and forget none of His benefits.*

PSALM 103:1-2

Two of the greatest words in the English language are *thank you*. At an early age we begin to teach our children to say, "Thank you." When someone gives them a gift or a compliment—and before they can even utter the words, we jump right in and remind them, "Now what do you say?" However, as we grow from childhood to adulthood we often forget our manners and hold back from expressing our appreciation to someone who does us a service.

It's the same way with God. He loves to hear and know we are thankful for all He bestows upon us. He is the provider of all we have. In Ecclesiastes 2:24-25 we read,

> There is nothing better for a man than to eat and drink and tell himself that his labor is good. This also I have seen, that it is from the hand of God. For who can eat and who can have enjoyment without Him?

Thankful hearts give thanks. One way to express our thanks for our food is to give a blessing each time we have a meal. Our family always gives a blessing of grace before we eat. This is a tradition at home or out at a restaurant. We never want to forget where our food comes from. We never want to take for granted the food we regularly have.

As I've gotten older, I look back over this short life and realize that God has been faithful all along the way. He has always provided for all our "needs." Not necessarily for our "wants," but for our "needs." That's totally in keeping with the words of 2 Peter 1:3:

> His divine power has granted to us everything pertaining to life and godliness, through the true knowledge of Him who called us by His own glory and excellence.

The password for entering into God's presence is "Thank You":

> Enter His gates with thanksgiving, and His courts with praise, give thanks to Him; bless His name (Psalm 100:4).

We humbly reach out to God with thanksgiving and praise. One of the leading indicators of our spiritual walk with God is our thankfulness for all He has done for us. Paul shares with us in Romans 1:21 about the human condition:

> Even though they knew God, they did not honor Him as God, or give thanks; but they became futile in their speculations, and their foolish heart was darkened.

This verse should be a red flag for us men. It's a warning that if we forget who God is, our foolish hearts will be darkened. Oh, no, not all at once, but small decisions over a period of time will lead us away from our God. We must guard our hearts so they don't turn inward—so, rather, that our heartbeats lead us away from ourselves and toward others.

Paul in his writings told us to be content in all situations (Philippians 4:11). When we're restless and find ourselves discontent with our lives and our situations, it's accentuated when we don't have a heart that readily gives thanks.

> In everything give thanks; for this is God's will for
> you in Christ Jesus (1 Thessalonians 5:18).

Let's not take anything for granted. The big things are easy to recall, because they are the biggies; the things like air, water, home, wife, food, children, and so on are often overlooked because we just assume they are there. In *everything* give thanks.

 Prayer

Father God, don't let me forget to always be thankful for what You do for me. You are a gracious God who continually pours out blessings on my life. Thank You for everything—big and small. Amen.

 Action

ACTION

Evaluate the thankfulness of your heart. How could it be improved?

Today's Wisdom

"To be thankful for what I have received, and for what my Lord has prepared, is the surest way to receive more."

ANDREW MURRAY

The Symbol of the Cross

You who are going to destroy the temple and rebuild it in three days, save Yourself! If You are the Son of God, come down from the cross.

MATTHEW 27:40

I n the first century the cross needed no explanation, for the Jews had seen many of their countrymen crucified by the Romans. Early followers of Jesus were crucified on a cross. Over the centuries the cross has become the symbol for Christian belief. As the Star of David signifies the Jewish believer, so does the cross represent a Christian believer.

Designers of fine jewelry have fashioned beautiful necklaces in the shape of the cross. On mountaintops we see a cross erected as a symbol of Christianity. We journey to a military cemetery and see the graves marked with a white cross. Most Christian churches have steeples with a cross perched on top of the building.

What has this symbol given to us as believers? Well, for starters...

- no condemnation (Romans 8:1)
- freedom (8:2)

- has destroyed sin (8:3)
- forgiveness (8:3)
- life and peace (8:6)
- eternal life (8:10)
- acceptance (8:14)
- God's child (8:16)

Without the cross and the resurrection there would be nothing to have faith in. Our hope and assurance of salvation would be like a puff of air. It would offer no more than any other religious teaching. Without the cross it would be foolish for us to believe.

We must make a decision every day to follow after the cross of Jesus. In Matthew 16:24 we read, "Jesus said to His disciples, 'If anyone wishes to come after Me, he must deny himself, and take up his cross and follow Me.'"

Jesus knew that following Him would come with a price— that, as individuals, we would have to choose to follow Him, that He would not force you or me to be His servant, even though new life is given as a free gift to those who choose to serve Him.

"The word of the cross is to those who are perishing foolishness, but to us who are being saved it is the power of God" (1 Corinthians 1:18). In this verse Paul shows that worldly wisdom, which the Corinthians prized so highly, is the very antithesis of the wisdom of God. The world says the cross is foolish, but the Christian believer recognizes its message as the very power of God.

The cross assures us of eternal life. The following verses attest to...

- the hope of eternal life (Titus 1:2)
- the assurance of eternal life (1 John 5:13)
- the invitation to believe (John 5:24)

The cross is far more than a symbol. Throughout Christian history it's been the one sign of unity that bonds all believers together. The cross has come under attack by all who want to destroy the message of Jesus. Even today some of our governmental agencies have attempted to take all crosses from our governmental buildings. The world doesn't want any reminders of our Christian heritage. But what God has preserved for 2000 years He is able to maintain until He returns for the church.

Prayer

Father God, may I see more than just a symbol when I see the cross. May I appreciate what Your Son has done for me as a sinner. Without the cross and the resurrection there would be no Christian faith. Thank You for the cross. Amen.

Action

When you see a cross, remember what it represents and the price that Jesus paid for us.

Today's Wisdom

"Life doesn't begin at twenty, or at forty, but at the cross of Calvary."

ELAINE KILGORE

Emergency Phone Numbers

O Lord, hear me praying; listen to
my plea, O God my King, for I will
never pray to anyone but you.

PSALM 5:1 TLB

We live in a time when we need to have lists of all kinds of phone numbers. One for the plumber, one for the electrician, one for the handyman, one for the doctor, one for the fire department, and so on. At times, though, there are emergency calls we need to make that don't require a phone to connect. The numbers for those calls are found in the Bible.

Emergency Phone Numbers
- When in sorrow...call John 14.
- When men fail you...call Psalm 27.
- If you want to be fruitful...call John 15.
- When you have sinned...call Psalm 51.
- When you worry...call Matthew 6:19-34.
- When you are in danger...call Psalm 91.
- When God seems far away...call Psalm 139.

- When your faith needs stirring...call Hebrews 11.
- When you are lonely and fearful...call Psalm 23.
- When you grow bitter and critical...call 1 Corinthians 13.
- For Paul's secret to happiness...call Colossians 3:12-17.
- For an understanding of Christianity...call 2 Corinthians 5:15-19.
- When you feel down and out...call Romans 8:31.
- When you want peace and rest...call Matthew 11:25-30.
- When the world seems bigger than God...call Psalm 90.
- When you want Christian assurance...call Romans 8:1-30.
- When you leave home for labor or travel...call Psalm 121.
- When your prayers grow narrow or selfish...call Psalm 67.
- For a great invention/opportunity...call Isaiah 55.
- When you want courage for a task...call Joshua 1.
- For how to get along with fellow men...call Romans 12.
- When you think of investments and returns...call Mark 10.
- If you are depressed...call Psalm 27.
- If your pocketbook is empty...call Psalm 37.
- If you are losing confidence in people...call 1 Corinthians 13.
- If people seem unkind...call John 15.

- If you are discouraged about your work...call Psalm 126.
- If you find the world growing small and yourself great...call Psalm 19.

Alternate numbers
- For dealing with fear...call Psalm 34:7.
- For security...call Psalm 121:3.
- For assurance...call Mark 8:35.
- For reassurance...call Psalm 145:18.

Emergency numbers may be dialed direct. No operator assistance is necessary. All lines to heaven are open 24 hours a day and seven days a week.[16]

 ## Prayer

Father God, You say to call on You; that You will never forsake me. Thank You for giving me the Bible so I can be encouraged in any times of emergency. Amen.

 ## Action

Call one of the emergency phone numbers today to see what information you receive.

 ## Today's Wisdom

"Without wise leadership, a nation is in trouble; but with good counselors there is safety."

PROVERBS 11:14 TLB

Life is an opportunity, benefit from it.

Life is beauty, admire it.

Life is bliss, taste it.

Life is a dream, realize it.

Life is a challenge, meet it.

Life is a duty, complete it.

Life is a game, play it.

Life is a promise, fulfill it.

Life is sorrow, overcome it.

Life is a song, sing it.

Life is a struggle, accept it.

Life is a tragedy, confront it.

Life is an adventure, dare it.

Life is luck, make it.

Life is too precious, do not destroy it.

Life is life, fight for it.

ATTRIBUTED TO MOTHER TERESA

We All Need Friends

*A man of many friends comes
to ruin, but there is a friend who
sticks closer than a brother.*

PROVERBS 18:24

Paraphrased the above verse might read, "A man of too many friends will be broken in pieces. Indiscriminately chosen friends may bring trouble, but a genuine friend sticks with you through thick and thin."[17]

What a warning to us regarding friendship. Often we're challenged to have a lot of friends—however, *this* warning is to not have too many of the wrong friends. Over my lifetime I have been fortunate to have some great "2 AM" friends (ones who will be at your doorstep at 2 AM in the morning if you need them).

I have also had some great "seasonal friends"—ones who have come into my life for a short period of time or for a specific purpose and then fade away. Regardless of why friends enter your life, be blessed by the friends that come your way.

Recently I received one of those forwarded e-mails that dealt with this subject of friends:

People come into your life for a *reason*, a *season*, or a *lifetime*. When you know which one it is for a person, you will know what to do for that person.

When someone is in your life for a *reason*, it is usually to meet a need you have expressed. They have come to assist you through a difficulty, to provide you with guidance and support, to aid you physically, emotionally, or spiritually. They may seem like a godsend, and they are! They are there for the reason you need them to be. Then without any wrongdoing on your part, or at an inconvenient time, this person will say or do something to bring the relationship to an end. Sometimes they die. Sometimes they walk away. Sometimes they act up and force you to take a stand. What we must realize is that our need has been met, our desire fulfilled, their work is done. The prayer you sent up has been answered, and now it is time to move on.

Some people come into your life for a *season*, because your turn has come to share, grow, or learn. They bring you an experience of peace or make you laugh. They may teach you something you have never done. They usually give you an unbelievable amount of joy. Believe it! It is real! But only for a season.

If you are truly blessed you will have *lifetime* relationships that teach you lifetime lessons: things you must build upon in order to have a solid emotional foundation. Your job is to accept the lesson, love the person, and put what you have learned to use in all other relationships of your life. It is said that love is blind but friendship is clairvoyant (keen perception or insight).[18]

Regardless of how friends have come to me I appreciate the role they have played in my life. With the exception of my wife, Emilie, it is my friends who have helped me become the man I am. I cannot imagine living life without great male friends.

Prayer

Father God, thanks for bringing into my life men who have supported and encouraged me, and have corrected my blind spots. Those men have made a great contribution to my life. Amen.

Action

Call or write a note to your "2 AM" friends and tell them how much they mean to you.

Today's Wisdom

"The older I grow in years, the more the wonder and the joy increase when I see the power of these words of Jesus—'I have called you friends'—to move the human heart. That one word 'friend' breaks down each barrier of reserve, and we have boldness in his presence. Our hearts go out in love to meet his love."

CHARLES F. ANDREWS

Choose Love

Saying "Yes!" to God is not a simple matter because making our lives into lives of love is not a simple or easy thing. To choose love as a life principle means that my basic mindset or question must be: What is the loving thing to be, to do, to say? My consistent response to each of life's events, to each person who enters and touches my life, to each demand on my time and nerves and heart, must somehow be transformed into an act of love. However, in the last analysis, it is this "Yes!" that opens me to God. Choosing love as a life principle widens the chalice of my soul, so that God can pour into me His gifts and graces and powers.

JOHN POWELL

Being a Man of Honor

*Be devoted to one another in brotherly love;
give preference to one another in honor.*

ROMANS 12:10

There are many men who spend their whole lives trying to gain the attention and honor of others. We volunteer, we spend hours in community efforts, we move from one head office to another, we become chairmen of all kinds of organizations and committees hoping to gain some honor—a watch, a plaque, a raise in salary, stock options—on and on. We are men who continue to strive for that golden award called *honor*.

Some of our attempts are legal, some are illegal, and some may be legal but are not aboveboard. Some of us are willing to cross the line of proper behavior and do what we know is wrong.

All throughout Scripture, though, we read passages that uphold honor and exhort us to be men of honor:

- honor your father and mother (Exodus 20:12)
- honor the aged (Leviticus 19:32)

- before honor comes humility (Proverbs 15:33)
- don't seek honor from men (Matthew 6:2)
- let marriage be held in honor (Hebrews 13:4)

In the book of Psalms we read of David's struggle with his enemies and his God. David was a man of dishonor in many phases of his life, but he was also described as "a man after God's own heart." He represents the struggles we have as men—tossed by the world and rescued by God. One of my favorite psalms is Psalm 15. Here David lists 11 attributes of an honorable man—one who can reside in the Lord's tent:

1. he walks with integrity (verse 2)
2. he works righteousness (verse 2)
3. he speaks truth in his heart (verse 2)
4. he does not slander with his tongue (verse 3)
5. he does not do evil to his neighbor (verse 3)
6. he does not take up a reproach against a friend (verse 3)
7. he despises a reprobate [a corrupt person] (verse 4)
8. he honors those who fear the Lord (verse 4)
9. he swears to his own hurt (even when the truth will hurt him), and does not change (verse 4)
10. he does not put out his money at [high] interest (verse 5)
11. he does not take a bribe against the innocent (verse 5)

Such a man as this will stand firm forever. A man of honor will surprise the world. In many cases the world will think a man of honor to be foolish. They simply cannot understand the ways of an honorable man.

However, this is the kind of man in whom God will exalt. To be a man of honor is to be one who is *faithful*. And what is the prize for being honorable?

> In the future there is laid up for me the crown of righteousness which the Lord, the righteous Judge will award to me on that day; and not only to me, but also to all who have loved His appearing (2 Timothy 4:8).

If honors come your way, accept them, realizing they are only temporal. God is the One who will bestow eternal honors on us. The greatest honor we will ever receive is when Jesus says, "Enter in—well done, My good and faithful servant."

Prayer

Father God, I want to be a man of honor—one who is faithful as a husband, a father, a worker, and a citizen. I want to be known as a man after God's own heart. Help me to be that man of honor. Amen.

Action

Review your life to see if there is anything about you that is preventing you from being a man of honor. If so, what are you going to do about it?

Today's Wisdom

"When one has to seek the honor that comes from God only, he will take the withholding of the honor that comes from men very quietly indeed."

GEORGE MACDONALD

Hear the Bells

*Ascribe to the LORD the glory due to His
name; worship the LORD in holy array.*

PSALM 29:2

A young man from a west Texas farm community received a football scholarship from a small college in Texas. He was very excited about this new adventure. After he had packed his bags to take to school, his mother said goodbye. After her hugs and tears she asked her son to make her one promise. "Be sure to attend church every Sunday while you are away from home." With no hesitation he assured his mama he would honor that request.

After settling into his dorm, he met several incoming freshmen he liked. However, these young men had few if any spiritual interests. One of the boys came from a wealthy farm family nearby, and he invited his new friends to come home with him for the weekend to hunt and fish. Of course, the small-town farm boy said, "Yes, that will be fun."

On Sunday morning as they were mounting their horses to go where the hunting and fishing were good, the young man heard the loud bell ring from a nearby church. They rode on farther toward their day's adventure, when again the young man heard a fainter ringing of the church bells. Going farther toward their destination and farther from the church bells, this young man again heard the church bells ring, but this time the sound was very faint. He stopped his horse and told his host he had to go back and attend church. The host said, "We don't have to go to church today. Let's go on and I will go to church with you next week." The young man replied, "No, I must go back while I can still hear the bell!"

Are you in that young man's situation—where you once heard God's strong voice, but today you have moved away from God and His voice is no longer strong but has become fainter and fainter? Your conscience might be calling out, *Go back while you can still hear the voice of God!*

If you feel far away from God, guess who moved? Return to Him before you no longer hear His voice calling you to come back home.

Prayer

Father God, continue to ring the bell loud and clear. I never want to stop hearing Your call. May everything that would hinder me from hearing Your voice be silenced. Amen.

ACTION

Action

How clear do you hear the bell ring? If it's not clear, you will want to turn back again to your first love.

Today's Wisdom

"Worship depends not upon our own activities, but upon the activities which God brings to bear upon us; to them we are forced to react as worshipers."

KENNETH E. KIRK

Rules for Daily Life

Begin the day with God
Kneel down to Him in prayer;
Lift up thy heart to His abode,
And seek His love to share.

Open the book of God
And read a portion there;
That it may hallow all thy thoughts,
And sweeten all thy care.

Go through the day with God
Whate'er thy work may be;
Where'er thou art—at home, abroad,
He still is near to thee.

Converse in mind with God
Thy spirit heavenward raise:
Acknowledge every good bestowed,
And offer grateful praise.

Conclude the day with God
Thy sins to Him confess;
Trust in the Lord's atoning blood,
And plead His righteousness.

Lie down at night with God
Who gives His servants sleep;
And when thou tread'st the vale of death,
He will thee guard and keep.[19]

The Making
of a Home

Unless the LORD builds the house,
they labor in vain who build it.

PSALM 127:1

As a young dad I sometimes wondered if we actually had a home—or was it merely a stopover place to eat, do laundry, hang around, and sleep? Was it just a place to repair broken objects, mow the lawn, pay off the mortgage, paint, wallpaper, install new carpet, and buy new furniture?

I finally figured out that a real home is much more than all that; it's a place where people live together, grow, die, laugh, cry, learn, and create together.

After watching his house burn down, a small child was once quoted as saying, "We still have a home. We just don't have a house to put it in." He understood what a home really was.

Our home should be a trauma center for the whole family. We don't have to be perfect—just forgiven. Everywhere else—school, work, neighborhood, church—people expect us to be perfect. Our home is a place where we can be ourselves. We all need a place to be just us, with no pretense. We can laugh

117

when we feel like it and cry when we need to. We can grow, we can make mistakes, we can agree, and we can disagree. Home should be a place where happy experiences occur—a place sheltered from the problems of the world and a place of love, acceptance, and security.

When we read the morning newspaper, we are confronted with all the tragedies around us. We realize the world outside our front door is falling apart, but within our four walls we can offer a place called *home*.

What can we as dads do to have a home like God intended? As with everything in life, when something is broken we go back to the instruction manual.

In this case it's the Bible. The home is God's idea—not something invented by twenty-first-century Americans. In the original plan of creation God designed the home to be the foundation of society—a place to meet the mental, spiritual, physical, and emotional needs of people.

Scripture states that marriage is a permanent relationship not to be divided (Mark 10:9). Marriage is instituted by God to accomplish His plans in our society. In marriage a husband and wife become "one" (Genesis 2:24), building a permanent relationship. It's not a temporary convenience to be maintained as long as it feels good. God designed the family as an enduring relationship in which, with His care, humans could weather the storms of life together. The home is God's loving shelter for growing to maturity.

"Unless the Lord builds the house, they labor in vain who build it." God is not only the designer, but He also wants to take the headship of family life. He wants to guide and to give love, peace, and forgiveness abundantly.

Solomon spoke to this subject in Proverbs 24:3-4:

> By wisdom a house is built, and through under-
> standing it is established; through knowledge its

rooms are filled with rare and beautiful treasures (NIV).

We've got our work cut out for us if we want a true home. We must live life with a big purpose—to have not just a house but a home.

Prayer

Father God, You know I want our house to be more than just a place—I want it to be a home. I want to yield to Your leadership. Give me wisdom, understanding, and knowledge. Amen.

ACTION

Action

Pray for your home and its various members.

GET WISDOM

Today's Wisdom

Try, Try Again

'Tis a lesson you should heed,
Try, try again;
If at first you don't succeed,
Try, try again;
Then your courage should appear,
For, if you will persevere,
You will conquer, never fear;
Try, try again.

Once or twice though you should fail,
Try, try again;
If you would at last prevail,
Try, try again;

If we strive, 'tis no disgrace
Though we do not win the race;
What should you do in this case?
Try, try again.

Time will bring you your reward,
Try, try again.
All that other folks can do,
Why, with patience, should not you?
Only keep this rule in view;
Try, try again.

W.E. HICKSON (1803–1870)

You Are Worth More Than a Sparrow

You are more valuable than many sparrows.

LUKE 12:7

In today's world, people have put the same value on animals as on human beings. A high percentage of college students would rescue a dog from drowning first over a mediocre man. We don't get it.

Genesis 1:26 tells us,

> God said, "Let Us make man in Our image, according to Our likeness; and let them rule over the fish of the sea and over the birds of the sky and over the cattle and over all the earth, and over every creeping thing that creeps on the earth...."

Jesus of Nazareth must have been a bird watcher of sorts because He frequently referred to bird life in His sermons:

- "Are not two sparrows sold for a cent? And yet not one of them will fall to the ground apart from the Father" (Matthew 10:29).

- "Look at the birds of the air; that they do not sow, neither do they reap, nor gather into barns, and yet your heavenly Father feeds them. Are you not worth much more than they?" (Matthew 6:26).

- "The very hairs of your head are all numbered. Do not fear; you are of more value than many sparrows" (Luke 12:7).

One of the favorite old hymns, "His Eye Is on the Sparrow," written by Civilla D. Martin, deals with this theme. She gave this account of the writing of this song:

> Early in the spring of 1905, my husband and I were sojourning in Elmira, New York. We contracted a deep friendship for a couple by the name of Mr. and Mrs. Doolittle—true saints of God. Mrs. Doolittle had been bedridden for nigh twenty years. Her husband was in incurable cripple who had to propel himself to and from his business in a wheelchair. Despite their afflictions, they lived happy Christian lives, bringing inspiration and comfort to all who knew them. One day while we were visiting with the Doolittles, my husband commented on their bright hopefulness and asked them for the secret of it. Mrs. Doolittle's reply was simple: "His eye is on the sparrow, and I know He watches me." The beauty of this simple expression of boundless faith gripped the hearts and fired the imagination of Dr. Martin and me. The hymn "His Eye Is on the Sparrow" was the outcome of that experience.[20]

The words of the song are as follows:

> Why should I feel discouraged?
> Why should the shadows come?
> Why should my heart be lonely

And long for heaven and home
When Jesus is my portion?
My constant friend is He:
His eye is on the sparrow,
And I know He watches me;
His eye is on the sparrow,
And I know He watches me.

Whenever I am tempted,
Whenever clouds arise,
When song gives place to sighing,
When hope within me dies,
I draw the closer to Him,
From care He sets me free;
His eye is on the sparrow,
And I know He watches me;
His eye is on the sparrow,
And I know He watches me.

What a joy to know that if God watches over the sparrow He certainly will watch over us, who were created in His image.

Eighty-five percent of the things we worry about never happen. One of man's weaknesses is that we don't have enough faith to trust God with our concerns. Over the years Emilie and I have adopted Matthew 6:33 as our life theme verse: "Seek first His kingdom and His righteousness and all these things shall be added to you."

The phrase "all these things" literally means everything—food, shelter, family, clothing, or your body. Scripture assures us not to worry about these things. The next verse tells us, "Do not be anxious for tomorrow; for tomorrow will care for itself. Each day has enough trouble of its own."

God is definitely interested in all our cares. If He takes care of the birds of the air, He certainly will take care of our smallest needs.

 Prayer

Father God, You are a God who cares for my littlest concerns. Let me always remember the little sparrow when I take things away from You and try to handle them myself. Amen.

 Action

Cast your worries on the Lord. This is a wonderful faith-builder.

 Today's Wisdom

"Are you looking unto Jesus now, in the immediate matter that is pressing, and receiving from him peace? If so, he will be a gracious benediction of peace in and through you. But if you try to worry it out, you obliterate him and deserve all you get."

OSWALD CHAMBERS

God Is Bound by His Promises

Keep watching and praying, that you may not enter into temptation; the spirit is willing, but the flesh is weak.

MATTHEW 26:41

God always keeps His promises. His character will not let Him fall back. In truth, all prayers offered through His Son, Jesus, are bound to be heard. God finds joy in keeping His promises.

We live in a day where all aspects of life are being undermined by dishonesty. Families have lost most of their retirement funds because they believed executives' promises that were made with their fingers crossed behind their backs.

Oh, how desperate our country is for people with character! We look to our sports heroes, our political leaders, our corporate leadership, the stars of movies and television, and even our spiritual leaders, hoping they will show us how people of character live. Each time we feel comfortable that a certain personality has the answer, we are disappointed by some revelation of broken dreams and promises.

We expect people to do what they say they are going to do. We are disappointed when a plumber, an electrician, a painter, or a co-worker can't do what they've said they are going to do. They miss the appointment or don't deliver their product on time—and here we patiently wait and nothing happens. Even parents tell their children that such-and-such will happen on Saturday, and it doesn't happen as promised. How many children go to their rooms to cry because a promise was broken?

We are so thankful we have One who never goes back on His promises. God the Father, Jesus the Son, and the Holy Spirit always keep Their word. If They said it, you can believe it. Let's all learn from the master of character to "just do what you say you are going to do."[21]

 Prayer

> Father God, thanks for being a promise-keeper. You are the model for every man who wants to be an honorable man. You give great confidence from Your Word because I know You won't break Your promise. If You said it, I believe it. Amen.

 Action

> Make and keep a promise to someone today—even a small one. Make this practice a discipline of your faith.

 Today's Wisdom

> "Now to the King eternal, immortal, invisible, the only God, be honor and glory forever and ever. Amen."
>
> 1 TIMOTHY 1:17

It Hurts to Be Right

*Blessed are those who have been
persecuted for the sake of righteousness,
for theirs is the kingdom of heaven.*

MATTHEW 5:10

This verse is taken from Jesus' Sermon on the Mount, a detailed revelation of the righteousness of God. Its principles are applicable to the children of God today. The nine Beatitudes (the "blessed" verses) in the Sermon describe the inner condition of a follower in the future.

"Rejoice, and be glad, for your reward in heaven is great." Wow! What a promise. As men, we like to know what the bottom line is all about. In order to obtain a blessing there is always a condition. In this case we must be persecuted for the sake of righteousness. It takes a very brave man to stand up to persecution. The faint of heart need not apply. A prominent Christian once told me, "When I get a lot of criticism, then I know I'm on the right track. Something good is happening."

Yes, it truly hurts to be right. Why do these hurts come?

There's a difference in our value system:

- "If the world hates you, you know that it has hated Me before it hated you" (John 15:18).

- "All who desire to live godly in Christ Jesus will be persecuted" (2 Timothy 3:12).

- "He thought it was better to suffer for the sake of the Messiah than to own the treasures of Egypt, for he was looking ahead to the great reward that God would give him" (Hebrews 11:26 NLT).

We are moral irritants to the world:

- "They are surprised that you do not run with them into the same excess of dissipation, and they malign [say bad things about] you" (1 Peter 4:4).

We are a wonder to those around us:

- "If anyone suffers as a Christian, let him not feel ashamed, but in that name let him glorify God" (1 Peter 4:16).

Sometimes life just hurts:

- "These things I have spoken to you, so that in Me you may have peace. In the world you have tribulation [trials and sorrows], but take courage; I have overcome the world" (John 16:33).

We see red stop signs all through life. The Word says,

- "The world would love you if you belonged to it" (John 15:19 NLT).

- "If your aim is to enjoy this world, you can't be a friend of God" (James 4:4 NLT).

For many years I tried to straddle the fence. One foot on the Christian side and the other foot in a compromising world.

I found I was only marginally successful on both sides of the fence—lukewarm in each.

Over time and after much study, much time in a strong men's support group, and much fervent prayer from my wife, I said, "This isn't working out as I planned." Rather than going through the usual midlife crisis, I put both feet into my spiritual dimension of life. What a difference this choice has made for me. Many of my old friends are no longer in my life, but the quality of my new friends is so encouraging to me.

Jesus' words in Mark 10:29-30 came alive to me during this time:

> Truly I say to you, there is no one who has left house or brothers or sisters or mother or father or children or farms, for My sake and for the gospel's sake, but that he shall receive a hundred times as much now in the present age, houses and brothers and sisters and mothers and children and farms, along with persecutions; and in the age to come, eternal life.

As men, what are we to do when it costs to be right?

Stand firm:

- "Resist him [Satan], firm in your faith, knowing that the same experiences of suffering are being accomplished by your brethren who are in the world. After you have suffered for a little while, the God of all grace, who called you to His eternal glory in Christ, will Himself perfect, confirm, strengthen and establish you" (1 Peter 5:9-10).

- "We...exult in our tribulations, knowing that tribulation brings about perseverance; and perseverance, proven character; and proven character, hope; and hope does not disappoint, because the love of God has been poured out within our hearts through the Holy Spirit who was given to us" (Romans 5:3-5).

Be glad:
- "Be very glad—because these trials will make you partners with Christ in his suffering" (1 Peter 4:13 NLT).

Look to the example of Jesus:
- "He was willing to die a shameful death on the cross because of the joy he knew would be his afterward" (Hebrews 12:2 NLT).

Yes, it hurts to be right. Don't think that life will always be rosy. There is suffering to be endured—but praise God that Scripture has been given to us to give us hope and His promises of our future blessings. My wife and I have realized we seldom grow during the "good times" of life. It is when we're weak we become strong. When these sufferings come (as they will), stand firm and be glad, because you know that there is growth just around the corner.

Prayer

Father God, You are a God who knows all about suffering. Your Son, Jesus, was our example as He went to the cross for our sins. Give me the power to stand firm during my times of suffering. Amen.

ACTION

Action

Turn your suffering into praises. Read James 1:1-4.

Today's Wisdom

"If suffering is accepted and lived *through*, not fought against and refused, then it is completed and becomes transmuted. It is absorbed, and having accomplished its work, it ceases to exist as suffering, and becomes part of our growing self."

ERIC GRAHAM HOWE AND
LILIAN LE MESURIER

When I say I am a Christian,
I am not shouting, "I am saved"

I'm whispering "I was lost,"
that's why I chose his way.

When I say I am a Christian,
I don't speak of this with pride

I'm confessing that I stumble,
needing God to be my guide.

When I say I am a Christian,
I'm not bragging of success

I'm admitting I have failed
and cannot ever pay the debt.

When I say I am a Christian,
I don't think I know it all

I submit to my confusion,
ask humbly to be taught.

When I say I am a Christian,
I'm not claiming to be perfect

My flaws are too visible,
but God believes I'm worth it.

When I say I am a Christian,
I do not wish to judge

I have no authority,
I only know I'm loved.

CAROL WIMNER

Who I Am in Christ

As many as received Him, to them He gave the right to become children of God, even to those who believe in His name.

JOHN 1:12

Who am I? This is a basic question we face in life. In reality there are two audiences that answer that question: First, others; and second, God. Man's opinion is short-lived and will soon fade away, but God's thoughts are eternal and will be everlasting.

Nothing is more freeing than agreeing with God about how He sees you and me. That's why it is so important to be in a daily study of God's Word. This exercise will offer us crucial understanding:

- we will know who God is
- we will know who we are in Him
- we will know what we have in Him
- we will know what we can do through Him

Day by day we are to live out who we are as new creations in Christ Jesus. The following alphabet is just the beginning of our relationship with God the Father, God the Son, and God the Holy Spirit:

Able to do all things (Philippians 4:13)
Becoming conformed to Christ (Romans 8:29)
Chosen (Colossians 3:12)
Delivered (2 Timothy 4:18)
Equipped (2 Timothy 3:17)
Filled with joy (John 17:13)
Guarded by God (2 Timothy 1:12)
Holy (Hebrews 10:10)
Instrument of righteousness (Romans 6:13)
Justified (1 Corinthians 6:11)
Known (2 Timothy 2:19)
Lacking no wisdom (James 1:5)
Made by Him (Psalm 100:3)
Never forsaken (Philippians 4:19)
Overcomer (1 John 5:4-5)
Partaker of grace (Philippians 1:7)
Qualified to share His inheritance (Colossians 1:12)
Receiver of the riches of God's grace (Ephesians 1:7)
Sealed by God with the Holy Spirit (Ephesians 1:13)
Transformed into His image (2 Corinthians 3:18)
Useful for His glory (Isaiah 43:7)
Valued (Matthew 6:26)
Walking in new life (Romans 6:4)
eXample (Ephesians 5:2)
Yielded to God (Romans 6:13)
Zeal for God (Romans 10:2)[22]

Just think of all the value we have in Christ! His Word says

I'm important and have worth in His eyes. No matter what man may think of me, I have eternal value:

- I am deeply loved
- I am complete in Him
- He made me special
- He made me beautiful in His sight
- I am pleasing to Him
- I am forgiven in Him
- He wants to have fellowship with me

 Prayer

Father God, no matter what I think of myself, Your Word tells me I'm more valuable than gold or silver. As I look in the mirror may I see Your face reflecting back to me. Thank You for loving me so much. Amen.

 Action

Each day go through one of the ABCs of who you are and study the reference Scripture.

 Today's Wisdom

"On the whole, God's love for us is a much safer subject to think about than our love for him. Nobody can always have devout feelings; and even if we could, feelings are not what God principally cares about. Christian love, either toward God or toward man, is an affair of the will. But the great thing to remember is that, though our feelings come and go, his love for us does not."

C.S. LEWIS

What Good Are Problems?

*We can rejoice...when we run into
problems and trials for we know that they
are good for us—they help us learn to be
patient. And patience develops strength
of character in us and helps us trust God
more each time we use it until finally our
hope and faith are strong and steady.*

ROMANS 5:3-4 TLB

The problems we face will either defeat us or develop us to be what God wants us to be. We often say to ourselves, *I certainly don't need this problem.* In reality it's just what we *do* need. Unfortunately, most people fail to see that God wants to use problems for good in our lives. Often we react to trials foolishly and resent our problems rather than pausing to consider what benefit they might bring. Over the years, I've learned several basic principles to help me understand what God's using my problems for.

To direct us. Sometimes God must light a fire under us to get us moving. Problems often point us in a new direction and motivate us to change. Is God trying to get our attention? Sometimes it takes a painful situation to make us change our ways.

Our family was certainly given new direction when Emilie was diagnosed with cancer. Our family was rocked with that news. We were experiencing a fairy-tale life. Our ministry had launched us into a very busy speaking and writing schedule, our children and grandchildren were doing fine in their lives. Then all of a sudden, BAM! The worst news was that Emilie had to go into immediate chemotherapy treatment and radiation for a large tumor in her stomach. At that moment, life was changed forever—never to be the same again.

As we now look back, that was good direction from God. We have met people, experienced events, written five books relating to that event, that never would have happened without that problem entering our lives. Problems certainly give direction to our lives.

To inspect us. Former First Lady Nancy Reagan shared this quote: "People are like tea bags—if you want to know what's inside them, just drop them into hot water." Has God ever tested your faith with a problem? What do problems reveal about us? James 1:2-3 tells us,

> Dear brothers, is your life full of difficulties and temptations? Then be happy, for when the way is rough, your patience has a chance to grow. So let it grow, and don't try to squirm out of your problems: For when your patience is finally in full bloom, then you will be ready for anything, strong in character, full and complete (TLB).

As an impatient man, I too have been inspected. Hours upon hours of waiting with Emilie for MRIs, CAT scans, blood draws; waiting for test results; starting over again after a certain procedure isn't effective—all this has caused me to look deep inside myself to see what I'm made of. Some of that enlightenment has been good and some has been shocking—I've had to make adjustments when some things have been exposed.

Yes, problems cause a man to inspect himself and find out who he really is.

To correct us. Some lessons we learn only through pain and failures. It's likely that when you were a child your parents told you not to touch a hot stove. But you probably learned not to by being burned. Sometimes we only learn the value of something—health, money, a relationship—by losing it.

> The punishment you gave me was the best thing that could have happened to me, for it taught me to pay attention to your laws. They are more valuable to me than millions in silver and gold! (Psalm 119:71-72 TLB).

One of the greatest corrections God has given us during this ordeal is to slow down and take time to smell the roses. We were too busy. God told us to slow down and listen to Him.

To protect us. A problem can be a blessing in disguise if it prevents us from being harmed by something more serious. In our case I'm not privileged to know what we might have experienced if our situation hadn't come about, but I'm sure of one thing—God had our best in His consideration. He has a master plan and is concerned about every event of our lives. We can sit back and live out one of our favorite verses:

> We know that all that happens to us is working for our good if we love God and are fitting into his plans (Romans 8:28 TLB).

To perfect us. Problems, when responded to correctly, are character-builders. God is far more interested in our character than our comfort. Our relationship to Him and our character are the only two things we're going to take with us into eternity. Yes, we can rejoice when we run into problems. They help us learn to be patient. God is at work in our lives even when we do not recognize it or understand it. But it's much easier and more profitable when we cooperate with God.

When we measure success in our lives, we measure not only our achievements, but lessons learned, lives touched, and moments shared along the way. Our problem has been rich in harvest.

 ## Prayer

Father God, let me have a fuller appreciation of how to handle my problems. Give me the faith, courage, and energy to see the long-term value of my problems. Thanks for caring for me. Amen.

 ## Action

ACTION

Turn your problems into a real learning experience.

 ## Today's Wisdom

GET WISDOM

"What you are is God's gift to you; what you do with yourself is your gift to God."

DANISH PROVERB

Starting Over

Because they do not change,
therefore they do not fear God.

PSALM 55:19 NKJV

Change denotes a making or becoming
distinctly different and implies a
radical transformation of character or
replacement with something else.

WEBSTER'S

How does a man change his ways? How does he start over? Perhaps you've come to a point in life where you have resolved you need a new beginning. You've decided you want to...

- lose some weight and inches
- quit smoking
- lead a healthier lifestyle
- start saving for your children's college education
- pay off your credit-card debts
- be more organized
- live a simpler life

It's said it takes only 21 days to form a new habit. Just 21 days. That's all. To make your habit a permanent part of your life, you just have to stick to it. *Don't give up.*

The five tools presented here will help you make that change.

Have a plan. I've always said, "If you fail to plan, you plan to fail." It sounds simple, but most of us don't take the time to write down on paper what we'll do to start over. A lot of people want to quit smoking. So they quit, cold turkey. That's their plan. However, most of us can't stop an old habit immediately and begin a new habit right away. It's a lot easier to succeed if we set an overall plan for ourselves to follow.

Visiting your primary-care doctor and letting him or her know of your plan to stop smoking could be beneficial to your success. Your doctor can give support and encouragement you will need along your journey to quit.

You will be more successful having a plan to follow than flying by the seat of your pants, hoping it will work out okay.

Set smaller goals. We often tend to have high expectations of ourselves, which can lead to very little follow-through. Many times we have other unresolved issues related to areas that we want to change. If it were easy to change, we would have done it a long time ago. In order to achieve these big-time goals, you must set "bite size" or smaller goals that will bring you closer to achieving your resolution of change.

Setting smaller goals is practicing for the bigger goal. It's taking action. These smaller goals help you build your strength and stamina to make changes that will lead you to succeed. Each day you are practicing small so you eventually reach your big goal.

Develop a support system. Find an individual or a group of men who will come alongside you to give that all-important encouragement to stick with it. Don't give up! You can do it! Words of encouragement give us the proper motivation to keep on going. Announce to the world what your goals are and ask others for support.

Finding a friend who has a similar goal can help tremendously. You can work together and support each other on your journey. All of us will hit the wall at some point in our starting over. Having someone to talk you through it or just listening can be invaluable. The two of you can share resources of information and check in on each other's progress.

Don't expect perfection. Expect setbacks along the way. No one is perfect, and if you expect perfection of yourself, you will be setting yourself up for failure. Instead, expect improvement from yourself and progress toward reaching your goal. When you do have a setback, get back on the horse and start over again—you will continually be moving forward.

Habits are hard to change. You've spent many years forming the old habits, so don't expect to change them overnight. Be committed to achieving your goal, no matter how long it takes. Don't let yourself get discouraged. Be willing to readjust your timeline as necessary.

> Consider it all joy, my brethren, when you encounter various trials, knowing that the testing of your faith produces endurance. And let endurance have its perfect result, so that you may be perfect and complete, lacking in nothing (James 1:2-4).

Have a reward. Be proud of your progress; reward yourself on a regular basis. Make a list of things you enjoy doing that can be classified as rewards. Here are some things you might consider:

- buy a new book
- buy a new CD or DVD
- play a round of golf or tennis

- go to a sporting event
- get a massage
- take your wife to a play
- join a gym
- take sailing lessons

Make your list personal and list only those things that give you pleasure. Think positive. Focus on the progress you are making, however small. Keep a "gratitude journal," where you list five things you are grateful for every day.

Prayer

Father God, help me start over in some areas of my life that need changing. With Your support I know I can do it. It seems like it is such a big effort, but I'm finally at a place in my life where I want to make changes. Amen.

Action

Write in your journal what changes you want to make, and list several things you are going to do to make those changes.

Today's Wisdom

"You can't change circumstances and you can't change other people, but God can change you."

Evelyn A. Thiessen

We Are Seasoners of Life

You are the salt of the earth.

MATTHEW 5:13

One of our favorite TV programs is *Emeril Live*. Emeril Lagasse is a very charismatic chef from New Orleans. In his food preparation, he is always talking about seasoning and "taking it a notch higher." When he throws in the seasoning he gives a very active arm and hand motion and utters a high-pitched "BAM" as the seasoning hits the food.

For Emeril seasoning food is key. And his fans love his theatrics, letting out an enthusiastic cheer when he takes it "a notch higher" and utters his classic "BAM!" They all know that food without seasoning is bland and less appealing to the fine diner.

That's the way it is in our Christian life too. If we are bland and have no flavor, no one will want to follow our recipe for life. Jesus tells us that we are to be the salt of the earth. We are to be seasoners of life to all those we meet in this decaying world.

Some time ago, before Hurricane Katrina hit in 2005, Emilie and I spent five days in New Orleans. After seeing Bourbon Street in the French Quarter—a section of town only tourists visit—we agreed this area well represented the dark and decaying elements of life. It was just this sort of decay and decadence that Jesus saved us from. As we saw the darkness there, we both said, "Thank You, Jesus, for what You did for us on the cross."

There is a difference between Christ-followers and the world:

> We all, with unveiled face, beholding as in a mirror
> the glory of the Lord, are being transformed into
> the same image from glory to glory, just as from the
> Lord, the Spirit (2 Corinthians 3:18).

As believers our faces reflect the spirit of the Lord. Our character is often the only Bible the unbeliever will ever read. Our countenance radiates that there is something different about us. Many times people will ask us, "Are you Christians?" When we say yes, they will reply, "I thought so—you seem to have a calmness the rest of the world doesn't have!"

Our call as Christian men is twofold:

- stand against moral decay and darkness
- bring light and seasoning to the outside world

Throughout Scripture Jesus shares that we are to be influencers of the world (rather than being influenced *by* the world):

- "Jesus spoke to them, saying, 'I am the Light of the world; he who follows Me will not walk in the darkness, but will have the Light of life' " (John 8:12).

- "Let your light shine before men in such a way that they may see your good works, and glorify your Father who is in heaven" (Matthew 5:16).

- "However you want people to treat you, so treat them, for this is the Law and the Prophets" (Matthew 7:12).

- "The whole Law is fulfilled in one word, in the statement, 'You shall love your neighbor as yourself'" (Galatians 5:14).

As seasoners of life, let's be reminded that one of our main purposes is to love, love, and love. Each time we shed light upon a family member, a neighbor, or a fellow worker we are showering God's love upon them. Whenever our lives reflect the love of God, our heavenly Father is glorified (Matthew 5:16).

 ## Prayer

Father God, thank You for impressing on me the importance of being a seasoner to those I come into contact with each day. I so want to reflect Your love to them. Continue to remind me I am the light and salt of the world. Amen.

 ## Action

Each time you pick up the salt and pepper shakers to season your food, may you be reminded that you are a seasoner of life.

 ## Today's Wisdom

"The deepest principle in human nature is the craving to be appreciated."

WILLIAM JAMES

There *Will* Be Storms in Life

Many are the afflictions of the righteous;
but the LORD delivers him out of them all.

PSALM 34:19

Never in the history of the U.S. did the state of Florida experience such a destructive assault in the form of hurricanes as in 2004. Emilie and I almost went through one of those storms while we were doing a seminar in Jacksonville, Florida. We were able to catch the last plane out before hurricane Jeanne hit the coast. If we had not caught that plane, we would have been reluctant captives for three days in this area. When we got home, we turned on our TV to catch up on the latest news. We grieved with those who had lost loved ones, businesses, homes, cars, and the contents of their homes.

The clean-up process was horrendous and required much money and effort. Millions of lives would never be the same, as was even more the case with hurricane Katrina in 2005.

But not every storm we face is a literal storm. During our lifetime, all of us will experience storms that are as devastating as these tragedies of nature. They may not be as evident as a hurricane, but when you experience them, they are just as real to you. Such storms can turn our lives around—can turn our dreams into hellish nightmares. These storms are called divorce, disease, death, betrayal, bankruptcy, ill health, abuse, adultery...all kinds of addiction.

What do we do when these storms hit our lives? Do we go to the newsstand and find a book or magazine that will help us get through them? Not really. In the first place, you won't find your answer at the newsstand. But the Christian can find help in Scripture, by heeding what God has to say:

God has a purpose for our lives.

- "We know that God causes all things to work together for good to those who love God, to those who are called according to His purpose" (Romans 8:28).

- "The word of the LORD is upright; and all His work is done in faithfulness" (Psalm 33:4).

- "All Scripture is inspired by God and profitable for teaching, for reproof, for correction, for training in righteousness; that the man of God may be adequate, equipped for every good work" (2 Timothy 3:16-17).

God is for you.

- "He is able...to save forever those who draw near to God through Him, since He always lives to make intercession for them" (Hebrews 7:25).

- "The LORD is near to all who call upon Him, to all who call upon Him in truth" (Psalm 145:18).

- "We do not know how to pray as we should, but

the Spirit Himself intercedes for us with groanings too deep for words" (Romans 8:26).

- "Let everyone who is godly pray to You in a time when You may be found" (Psalm 32:6).

- "You are my hiding place; You preserve me from trouble; You surround me with songs of deliverance" (Psalm 32:7-8).

- "Everyone who asks receives, and he who seeks finds, and to him who knocks it will be opened" (Matthew 7:8).

- "All things you ask in prayer, believing, you will receive" (Matthew 21:22).

We have God's presence. In Mark 6:47-48; John 9:1,35; and John 11:33-35, we read that Jesus was with each person in the storm. He did not leave them alone. In all of our storms of life He is always with us.

- "My presence shall go with you, and I will give you rest" (Exodus 33:14).

- "Be strong and courageous! Do not tremble or be dismayed, for the LORD your God is with you wherever you go" (Joshua 1:9).

- "I will never desert you, nor will I ever forsake you" (Hebrews 13:5).

We have the peace of God.

- "In my distress I called upon the LORD, and cried to my God for help. He heard my voice out of His temple, and my cry for help before Him came into His ears" (Psalm 18:6).

- "Why are you troubled, and why do doubts arise in your hearts?" (Luke 24:38).

- "Peace I leave with you; My peace I give to you; not as the world gives do I give to you. Do not let your heart be troubled, nor let it be fearful" (John 14:27).

- "He Himself is our peace" (Ephesians 2:14).

We have God's power.

- "You will receive power when the Holy Spirit has come upon you" (Acts 1:8).

- "My grace is sufficient for you, for power is perfected in weakness. Most gladly, therefore, I will rather boast about my weaknesses, that the power of Christ may dwell in me" (2 Corinthians 12:9).

- "God has not given us a spirit of timidity, but of power and love and discipline" (2 Timothy 1:7).

These five principles can help us when we encounter those storms that seem to knock our legs out from under us. Though the wind may be calm and the waves might be manageable, for certain what is calm now will be a storm later on. How will we respond when the storms occur?

Don't look down, don't look back, but look upward toward the heavens and ask God to give you a new vision and purpose for this event. In our family, when the storm crashes in our lives, we ask God this question: "What lesson are you trying to teach us in this experience?"

Don't keep what you learn from your storms to yourself. Be available to help someone else when their storm hits shore. Without storms in our lives, we can't help others when they experience their own storms.

Prayer

Father God, show me Your purpose for each of my storms. Let me learn something—if I don't, those storms will be of no value for my life. From Scripture and from experience I know You are always with me. Amen.

 ## Action

Write down in your journal an experience of peace you have had in a storm of your life. Read Paul's prayer in Ephesians 1:18-21.

 ## Today's Wisdom

"It is suffering and then glory. Not to have the suffering means not to have the glory."

Robert C. McQuilkin

A man is loved
Not for how tall
He stands,
But for how often
He bends
To help, comfort,
And teach.

AUTHOR UNKNOWN

Remember the Morning Watch

*Open my eyes to see wonderful
things in your Word.*

PSALM 119:18 TLB

I t was in 1882 on the campus of Cambridge University that
the world was first given the slogan "Remember the morning
watch."

Two students found their days loaded with studies,
lectures, and bull sessions. Enthusiasm and activity
were the order of the day. These dedicated men
soon discovered a flaw in their spiritual armor—a
small crack which, if not soon closed, would bring
disaster.

They sought an answer and came up with a
scheme they called the morning watch—a plan to
spend the first minutes of a new day alone with
God, praying and reading the Bible.

The morning watch "sealed the crack" in their
armor. It enshrined a truth so often obscured by
the pressure of ceaseless activity that it needs daily

rediscovery: to know God, it is necessary to spend consistent time with Him.

The idea caught fire. "A remarkable period of religious blessing" followed, and culminated in the departure of the Cambridge Seven, a band of prominent athletes and men of wealth and education, for missionary service. They gave up everything to go out to China for Christ.

But these men found that getting out of bed in time for the morning watch was as difficult as it was vital. One of them was determined to turn indolence into discipline. He invented an automatic, foolproof cure for laziness. It was a contraption set up by his bed: "The vibration of an alarm clock set fishing tackle in motion, and the sheets, clipped to the line, moved swiftly into the air off the sleeper's body."

That young man wanted to get up to meet his God!

The intimacy of communion with Christ must be recaptured in the morning quiet time. Call it what you want—the quiet time, personal devotions, the morning watch, or individual worship—these holy minutes at the start of each day explain the inner secret of Christianity. It's the golden thread that ties every great man of God together—from Moses to David Livingstone, the prophet Amos to Billy Graham—rich and poor, businessmen and military personnel. Every man who has ever become somebody for God has this at the core of his priorities: time alone with God![23]

Psalm 57:7 tells us, "O God, my heart is quiet and confident. No wonder I can sing your praises!" (TLB). This kind of heart gives us stability in a life that's constantly saying, "Faster, faster, hurry, hurry!" Few of us men have this kind of heart. One of our pleas is, "How do I find the time?"

One way to get started is make this morning watch a priority for your life. Put it on your daily planner (the same as for any appointment) and have your wife or a male friend hold you accountable for this commitment. Morning is a great time to meet God because it gives you a great start for the day. Some of us are morning people and some are late-evening people. You decide what the best time for you is.

Psalm 5:3 gives us motivation to meet God: "In the morning, O LORD, You will hear my voice; in the morning I will order my prayer to You and eagerly watch." What kind of structure might you have? Here's a suggestion:

1. *Pray for guidance* so that you focus and dedicate this time just for the two of you (see Psalm 148:1-5).

2. *Read a portion of Scripture.* If you are new to the faith you might begin with the book of John (see Psalm 119:18).

3. *Have a time for prayer.* You might want to use the word "ACTS" to remember what four areas to include:

   - **A**—*Adoration.* This segment is all about God. You love Him, you adore Him, you thank Him for all He's done for you. Reflect on who He is (read Lamentations 3:22-23).

   - **C**—*Confession.* You agree with God on what sins you have committed. You need to come to God with a clean heart (read Psalm 66:18).

   - **T**—*Thanksgiving.* Be specific in thanking God for all He has given you. Thank Him for your marriage, your family, your home, your pastor, your job, and so on. Even thank Him for your difficult times—after all, these are events that create growth in your life (read 1 Thessalonians 5:18).

- **S**—*Supplication.* Make your requests known to God. Remember to include requests for others, such as government officials, missionaries, students, believers in other countries (read Matthew 7:7).

Become a member of the morning watch. There are no membership forms to fill out or any monthly dues. It takes 21 days to start a new habit. Begin today and see how it will have a positive influence on the rest of the day—and transform your life.

 ## Prayer

Father God, I want to meet You the first thing in the morning watch. When the alarm goes off, let me jump out of bed and be on time for our appointment. Amen.

 ## Action

Start forming your new habit tomorrow morning.

 ## Today's Wisdom

"Spread out your petition before God, and then say, 'Thy will, not mine, be done.' The sweetest lesson I have learned in God's school is to let the Lord choose for me."

DWIGHT L. MOODY

Don't Run
on Emptiness

Elijah was a man with a nature like ours.

JAMES 5:17

Have you ever been at a large sporting event, with thousands of people yelling and screaming—and yet you felt like you were all alone with no one who cared? That feeling is very common to us men who are living in a merry-go-round world. So much noise, but so little caring.

Elijah was such a man. He was just like us—empty, with no purpose in life. In 1 Kings 19:1-18,

- he was threatened with his life (verse 2)
- he was afraid (verse 3)
- he requested that he might die (verse 4)
- an angel touched him and said, "Arise, eat" (verse 5)
- the Lord asked, "What are you doing here?" (verse 9)
- he was told to go stand on the mountain before the Lord (verse 11)

- there were strong winds, an earthquake, a fire, and a sound of gentle blowing (or a gentle whisper) (verse 12)

- he lamented, "I have done all the LORD has asked and I alone am left" (verse 14)

Yes, Elijah was as human as we are. He was threatened, he was alone, he wanted to die, he was confused, he wanted to give in and call it quits. But he didn't. He went to the top of the mountain, and he heard the sound of a gentle whisper. He could have sloughed it off—ignored the message—but he didn't. By wise counsel from the Lord, Elijah was assured that he wasn't done (verses 15-16); he wasn't alone (verse 16); he wasn't a failure (verse 18).

If you find yourself in that empty state like Elijah, you too can be assured you are not done, not alone, and not a failure. Listen to that gentle whisper and get back on track.

How does one get back on the right track? Scripture gives us four ways to get away so we can hear the whisper of God's voice:

1. *Find a quiet spot.* "In the early morning, while it was still dark, He [Jesus] arose and went out and departed to a lonely place and was praying there" (Mark 1:35).

2. *Have an honest heart.* "You will seek Me and find Me, when you search for Me with all your heart" (Jeremiah 29:12-13).

3. *Open your Bible.* "The word of God is living and active and sharper than any two-edged sword, and piercing as far as the division of soul and spirit, of both joints and marrow, and able to judge the thoughts and intentions of the heart" (Hebrews 4:12).

4. *Have a genuine friend.* "Let us consider how to stimulate one another to love and good deeds, not forsaking our own assembling together, as is the habit of some but, encouraging one another; and all the more, as you see the day drawing near" (Hebrews 10:24-25).

God does not mean our life to be empty. His plan is for us to live a full and abundant life (John 10:10). As Rick Warren puts it in the opening of his bestselling book *The Purpose-Driven Life:*

> It's not about you. The purpose of your life is far greater than your own personal fulfillment, your peace of mind, or even your happiness. It's far greater than your family, your career, or even your wildest dreams and ambitions. If you want to know why you were placed on this planet, you must begin with God. You were born by his purpose and for his purpose.[24]

God did not create you to be empty. Reach down, grab hold of your bootstraps, and lift up. You're not meant to be *under* the pile, but to be *on top* of it.

 Prayer

Father God, lift me out of a life of emptiness. You didn't make me to be there, and that's not where I will remain. With Your spirit and power I will arise above this phase of emptiness and live an abundant life. Thank You for giving me a gentle whisper. Amen.

Action

If you find yourself in an empty stage of life, take the four steps that are given and put them into action this week.

Today's Wisdom

"Blessed are those who trust in the LORD...They are like trees planted along a riverbank, with roots that reach deep into the water. Such trees are not bothered by the heat or worried by long months of drought. Their leaves stay green, and they go right on producing delicious fruit."

JEREMIAH 17:7-8 NLT

When Jesus
Seems Silent

*He stayed...two days longer in
the place where He was.*

JOHN 11:6

In John 11 we are introduced to two sisters, Mary and Martha. Their brother, Lazarus, was very sick and near to death; they sent word to Jesus to come quickly so He could heal him. They thought Jesus would come immediately, but they were so disappointed when He didn't drop everything and come quickly. Instead He waited for two days, and by the time He got to them in Bethany, Lazarus had died and was already buried.

Have you ever experienced the silence of God? You have called out—but it's evident to your eyes He isn't there. Why, you ask?

There have been two times when Emilie and I cried out for healing, but God was silent.

The first time was upon learning of Emilie's "big C"—cancer. We met with the elders of our church for the anointing of Emilie with oil. We had never experienced this type of service for ourselves and weren't quite sure what to expect. It was a beautiful and very spiritual experience. We left that event with high expectations. We knew God was going to heal Emilie immediately. With great anticipation we waited for one day, two days, three days, one week, two weeks, a whole month...and no healing. Why was God silent? We did what the Bible told us to do, but still there were no signs that God was listening.

The second experience came when we went to Seattle, Washington, to the Fred Hutchinson Cancer Research Center for a bone-marrow transplant. They had located a 23-year-old Canadian man who was an unrelated donor that matched Emilie's components. We were so excited again, with very high expectations for healing.

After being in Seattle for 30 days Emilie was finally given the donor's bone marrow. Again we just knew she was going to be immediately healed. For 85 long days of going to the clinic for blood tests and consultations with the staff, Emilie wasn't healed. Finally after 125 days we were released to go back home. No healing, but all the blood counts were moving in the right direction. What a day of rejoicing when we got on that airplane to take us back to Southern California even though, as far as we were concerned, God had delayed and was silent during this experience.

What did we learn from these two experiences? We began to understand the sound of God's silence. We began to realize what we wanted wasn't always what God wanted for our lives.

We wanted—immediate healing—not in two months or two years, but *now!* We all have agendas, and they are not always God's plan for our lives.

God wants—for us to trust Him more in our lives.

During this time of searching out what to do when God is silent in our lives we went back to John 11:4 and adopted it as one of our theme verses: "This sickness is not to end in death, but for the glory of God, so that the son of God may be glorified by it."

Then in verses 14-15, of John 11, Jesus "said to them plainly, 'Lazarus is dead, and I am glad for your sakes that I was not there, so that you may believe; but let us go to him.'"

Yes, God's timing and purpose are much different than ours. Many times in life we aren't able to comprehend God's thoughts. Sometimes when God is silent, His clock is still ticking. Silence doesn't mean inactivity on His part. He is still there, and His ultimate plan will be revealed in His appointed time. Charles Spurgeon would often pray: "Lord, don't give me anything that I have prayed for if it's not good for me. Only grant those petitions that are in Your plan for my life." This has become our battle cry because we have come to realize it's not good for God to give us everything we want.

As Lazarus was ultimately healed (even after he had been in his grave for four days), so was Emilie.

It has taken us a number of years to get to the quality of life we now have. Many times we couldn't see any healing, but God was with us along the way. Not always in our timing, but most assuredly in His timing. He was not silent—we just couldn't always hear Him speaking. We have found that at our most desperate times God is silent. But He will not leave you or forsake you. He is always there. We must not confuse His silence with His absence. He is always with us.

 Prayer

Father God, thank You for always being at our side. I so appreciate the assurance that You are with us even when You seem to delay. I want to set my watch to be the same as Your clock. Amen.

Action

Write in your journal a time when God seemed to be silent in your life. Now jot down what you have learned about God's perfect timing.

Today's Wisdom

"Your kingdom come. Your will be done, on earth as it is in heaven" (Matthew 6:10).

Complete

I love you, He knows
And creates all.

I love you, He promises
And provides a covenant.

I love you more, He sighs
And sends a Savior.

I love you, He cries
And gives Himself.

I love you still, His Spirit lives
And opens our hearts.

Love is complete
And it is God.

JANE E. LEBRUN

Anxiety—The Curse
of Modern Man

*I say to you, do not be anxious for your
life, as to what you shall eat, or what
you shall drink; nor for your body as to
what you shall put on. Is not life more
than food, and the body than clothing?*

MATTHEW 6:25

I don't know about where you live, but in Southern California we tend to lead anxious lives. Although we have it much easier than our fathers did, we certainly are much more uneasy about our life than our fathers were.

For instance, my dad never cared much about going out to eat at the latest in-vogue restaurant, or vacationing at the new island hotel with the larger pool than the previous one. He didn't work out to keep his abs in shape nor make sure he wore the latest hot logo on his shirts and sweaters. And he wanted a car that would run efficiently, but it didn't have to be the hottest brand on the market. (It could even be American-made.) And it didn't have to be an SUV or have four-wheel drive and a plush interior.

Yes, today there seems to be a lot of pressure to make sure we keep up with the latest trends in search of the perfect life.

Take a hard look at the message from the modern media and you'll see what I mean. Most of the advertisements try to persuade us that what we wear and what restaurants we eat at and the cars we drive will determine who we are.

Our modern culture has built itself around the mind-set that causes us as men to be more concerned over life's accommodations along life's journey than with our final destination.

Because of all these false messages, we may look good on the outside, but we have a vast emptiness on the inside. We have all the trimmings of life. We have the best-dressed families, the finest homes, great-paying jobs. We go to all the five-star resorts, our garages are filled with the finest cars, we have all the latest and finest sporting gear, but we find ourselves *anxious*. Inside, we aren't satisfied with who we have become.

We come to a stage in life where we realize this thing called life is more important than food, and the body is more important than what we wear. We come to realize that all these things don't satisfy the soul and have become cheap substitutes for spiritual wholeness and well-being.

When man loses sight of who God is and forgets to give Him honor, anxiety sets in and day-to-day living doesn't make sense. When we make *things* our goal in life and take our eyes off Jesus, we invariably will be disappointed. An anxious man needs to turn his eyes on Christ and worship Him. I have found that He has never failed me in my journey. He gives moderation and balance to my life.

One of our family's favorite verses is Matthew 6:33: "Seek first His kingdom and His righteousness, and all these things shall be added to you." Yes, this is the "anxiety breaker"—seek *first* His kingdom. Emilie and I try to make this verse our test for doing anything in life. With this decision that needs to be made, are we truly seeking His kingdom first—or are we doing it just for ourselves?

In John 16:33 we read, "These things I have spoken to you, so that in Me you may have peace. In the world you have tribulation, but take courage; I have overcome the world." God has promised us peace, but many of us choose anxiety instead. Possessions will never give us satisfaction in life.

We will never be the men God wants us to be until we heed His call: "Come to Me...and I will give you rest."

Let Christ help you overcome the anxieties of life. He will help you to...

- Stop chasing the temporal things of life. Seek the kingdom of God as it is revealed in Jesus. Cast all your cares on Him.

- Take your eyes off yourself and focus them on God first. Many of our anxieties are rooted in our self-centeredness.

- Spend most of your prayer time in praying for others. Keep yourself away from most of your prayers.

- Not continue to straddle the fence. Commit your total efforts and energy to Christ.

The Christian man wholeheartedly committed to Jesus Christ is the truly happy man. In Philippians 1:21 Paul says of such a life, "For to me, to live is Christ and to die is gain."

 Prayer

Father God, take my eyes off the things of the world. I realize life is more than possessions. I have had them, and they don't give purpose and meaning to my life. I want to focus on serving You all of my days. Give me the power and conviction to follow Your ways. Amen.

Action

Analyze what is making you anxious. What are you going to do about it? Write out what these anxieties are and what you will do to change each into peace.

Today's Wisdom

"Anxiety is the natural result when our hopes are centered in anything short of God and his will for us."

BILLY GRAHAM

Anger Management

Laying aside falsehoods, speak truth, each one of you with his neighbor, for we are members of one another. Be angry, and yet do not sin; do not let the sun go down on your anger, and do not give the devil an opportunity.

EPHESIANS 4:25-27

There is a lot of unhealthy anger among men in our culture. Every day the news is full of stories relating to the evidence of this anger. We read about brawls, rapes, stabbings, shootings, murder, and beatings. Men have not learned how to control or manage their God-given emotion of anger.

When anger comes to us, it's always an opportunity for us to experience victory or defeat. Which it is will depend on how we choose to react.

As a young man I witnessed how my father would lash out when he got angry. Even though he was a church-attending Christian, he would become violent if someone would cross his path. I never witnessed physical outbursts, but his voice level and choice of words were not gentleman-like. As a young man I said I didn't want to be like that. However, just because I said it didn't make me not have an anger problem. To this very day

I have to be aware that Satan would like to seduce me in this area of my emotional life.

In my early married life I began refereeing sporting events such as football, baseball, and basketball. As a result, I learned to take verbal abuse from the fans without being able to argue back. This activity was a great experience for me. It taught me how to be calm during confrontations. I learned I couldn't fight back or try to defend a certain call. This was anger management at the most intense for me.

A few months ago my daughter, Jenny, said, "Dad, you are a very calm and patient man—you never lose your cool." She was shocked when I explained to her how I've had to work all my life to control my temper and anger.

In Genesis 4:1-15 we can read how the improper reaction to anger can lead to the agony of defeat.

- "Cain became very angry and dejected" (verse 5 NLT).

- " 'Why are you angry?' the LORD asked him. 'Why do you look so dejected?' " (verse 6).

- " 'You will be accepted if you respond in the right way. But if you refuse to respond correctly, then watch out! Sin is waiting to attack and destroy you, and you must subdue it' " (verse 7 NLT).

- "Later Cain suggested to his brother, Abel, 'Let's go out into the fields.' And while they were there, Cain attacked and killed his brother" (verse 8 NLT).

Through these verses we can follow the downfall of Cain. He had anger toward his brother. He couldn't manage the fire that burned in his stomach, and he ended up murdering his very own brother.

We might say, "Oh, that would never happen to me. I could never kill because of my anger." Our prisons are full of inmates who at one time said the very same thing.

Another biblical narrative shows how one man, Joseph, took his potential anger and reacted in a godly fashion. In Genesis 50 we read how Joseph responded to his brothers, who had sold him into slavery.

- He broke down and wept when his brothers told him of his father's request for him to forgive his wayward brothers (verse 17).

- When his brothers came and fell down before him and said, "We are your servants" (verse 18), Joseph said to them, "Do not be afraid, for am I in God's place?" (verse 19).

- Finally Joseph said, "You meant evil against me, but God meant it for good in order to bring about this present result, to preserve many people alive" (verse 20).

Here was Joseph, a man who had been wronged, who had every reason to be angry with his brothers. But he took the higher road in dealing with his anger. He realized God had a master plan for his life—that God was able to take a wrong and make it into a right.

Anger is not a neutral emotion. Either you control it, or it will control you. You must determine this before anger comes—will you manage it like Cain or like Joseph? You alone must make that decision.

When we release our anger we are set free. Freedom reigns.

Prayer

Father God, let me be a Joseph as I deal with my anger. Let me realize that what was meant for evil against me, You meant for my good. Let me be able to control this emotion in a positive fashion. Amen.

 ## Action

Jot down some areas in your life that need mastering. Beside each one, list what you aim to do to control this weak emotional area of your life. Give this list to the Lord.

 ## Today's Wisdom

Verses to help you with anger:

- "A quick-tempered man acts foolishly, and a man of evil devices is hated" (Proverbs 14:17).

- "Cease from anger, and forsake wrath; do not fret, it leads only to evildoing" (Psalm 37:8).

- "If you are angry with someone, you are subject to judgment" (Matthew 5:21-22 NLT).

- "You must make allowance for each other's faults and forgive the person who offends you. Remember, the Lord forgave you, so you must forgive others" (Colossians 3:13 NLT).

- "If you are standing before the altar in the Temple, offering a sacrifice to God, and you suddenly remember that someone has something against you, leave your sacrifice there beside the altar. Go and be reconciled to that person. Then come and offer your sacrifice to God" (Matthew 5:23-24 NLT).

- "A gentle answer turns away wrath, but a harsh word stirs up anger" (Proverbs 15:1).

- "A wrathful man stirs up strife, but he who is slow to anger allays contention" (Proverbs 15:18 NKJV).

- "Let every one be quick to hear, slow to speak and slow to anger" (James 1:19).

- "The anger of man does not achieve the righteousness of God" (James 1:20).

Making a Decision of Faith

Today I am giving you a choice
between prosperity and disaster,
between life and death.

DEUTERONOMY 30:15 NLT

A soldier in the hospital found a tract by his bed with the hymn, "Will You Go?" Twice he read it, thought about it, and threw it down. The last time, he read it, thought about it and, taking his pencil, wrote deliberately on the margin,

> By the grace of God, I will try to go.
> John Waugh, Company G,
> Tenth Regiment, P.R.V.C.

That night he went to a prayer meeting, read his resolution, requested prayers for his salvation, and said, "I am not ashamed of Christ now; but I am ashamed of myself for having been so long ashamed of him."

The young soldier was killed a few months after. How timely his decision was!

As men we're continually making decisions that will determine our future. How we decide will play out throughout our life—in prosperity or disaster, in life and death.

We must be committed to God's Word and promises so that when these moments of choosing come we're able to make our decisions based upon our faith. On a daily basis we are confronted with these kinds of decisions. How we handle these choices determines our future.

Often they are big decisions that will affect our marriage, our family, our walk with the Lord, our business relations, and the development of our character.

At other times we might think the decisions we're making are so small that no one is even paying attention. But be aware: "All little decisions reap the consequences for the future." What starts out as a small spark can be flamed into a huge forest fire.

We men often have strong egos, and we've been known to falsely believe we are God and don't need any help from anyone, especially from God. Let me give you a little hint—we *aren't* God, and the sooner we realize that the better our decisions will be.

Why struggle all your life to find this out? Moses in Deuteronomy 4:35 states very clearly, "The LORD, He is God; there is no other besides Him."

Don't fall into false security by thinking you don't need anyone but yourself. Often we don't have all the information we might want, but faith means you don't have to have 100 percent of the information.

As humans we always want to know "What's in it for me?" God is faithful to give you a promise that has been true in my life:

> All will be well with you and your children. Then you will enjoy a long life in the land the LORD your God is giving you for all time (Deuteronomy 4:40 NLT).

Prayer

Father God, give me the faith to make those all important decisions that will determine my destiny. You know I want prosperity and life for me and my family. I realize I am responsible for making that decision—give me the wisdom to rely on Your Word for those decisions. Amen.

Action

Step out in faith today and make the decisions that will give you prosperity and life.

Today's Wisdom

A wise man makes decisions in his youth that a foolish man makes in his old age.

Don't Forget the Past

From childhood you have known the
sacred writings which are able to give
you the wisdom that leads to salvation
through faith which is in Christ Jesus.

2 TIMOTHY 3:15B

f I had my school days to relive, I would have concentrated more on history—not only American history, but also the history of the world. All throughout Scripture we are told to remember our past. We are the end result of all of our past, not only from history but from all of our ancestors.

I'm overwhelmed when I realize that all through history none of my ancestors have been killed by war or disease before having the opportunity to become a father to the next generation in my line. Oh, yes, some may have died *after* having sired the next generation, but none before. And when you consider all the men who *have* died in war or from a disease in their youth, before having the opportunity to father a child, truly the odds that you and I are here is one in many millions. We are here today because of a miracle of survival.

Because of this miracle we are here today—and not by accident. We are here for a purpose. Have you taken time to consider what this purpose might be?

In Scripture, we men are challenged not to forget what matters most. Paul writes in 2 Timothy 1:5-8,

> I remind you to kindle afresh the gift of God which is in you through the laying on of my hands. For God has not given us a spirit of timidity, but of power and love and discipline.

In these latter days we as believers will be called on to stand up and give witness to Jesus and what He has done through history. We are told that during the last days men will

- ignore God
- love stuff
- use people
- play religious games
- be boastful and proud
- see children being disobedient to parents
- be ungrateful
- consider nothing sacred

This is certainly a list for today. But every day I try to remember the lessons of history to remind myself to...

- *Follow the examples God has given:* "You know what I teach, Timothy, and how I live, and what my purpose in life is. You know my faith and how long I have suffered. You know my love and my patient endurance" (2 Timothy 3:10 NLT).

- *Remain in God's Word:* "You must remain faithful to the things you have been taught. You know they are true, for you know you can trust those who taught you. You have been taught the holy Scriptures from childhood, and they have given you the wisdom to receive the salvation that comes by trusting in Christ Jesus. All Scripture is inspired by God and is useful to teach us what is true and to make us realize what is wrong in our lives. It straightens us out and teaches us to do what is right. It is God's way of preparing us in every way, fully equipped for every good thing God wants us to do" (2 Timothy 3:14-17 NLT).

- *Complete my calling:* "Preach the word of God. Be persistent whether the time is favorable or not" (2 Timothy 4:2 NLT).

- *Remember who is at the finish line:* "Each of us will stand personally before the judgment seat of God. For the Scriptures say, 'As surely as I live,' says the Lord, 'every knee will bow to me and every tongue will confess allegiance to God.' Yes, each of us will have a personal account to God" (Romans 14:10-12 NLT).

We must not forget our past. Biblical history lets me rest assured that God has a master plan for all of history. Though we might not be able to figure out what that master plan is, we can still know that God's thoughts are bigger than our thoughts. I'm not capable of understanding every event in history, but because I know who God is, I can be at peace with all situations. I want to know my past so I can know the future.

 Prayer

Father God, give me a desire to know my history to better help me understand the present and trust You for the future. Give me a desire to search out and find my purpose in life. Amen.

Action

To better understand your purpose, read Rick Warren's book *The Purpose-Driven Life.*

Today's Wisdom

"Long before you were conceived by your parents, you were conceived in the mind of God."

RICK WARREN

Thank You, Lord

*I have learned to be content in
whatever circumstances I am.*

PHILIPPIANS 4:11

hy wait for Thanksgiving Day to be thankful? One day
a year is not enough. Every morning upon waking and
every evening before we nod off on our pillow these two words
need to come from our mouths: "Thank You."

A few years ago my wife, Emilie, and I wrote a book of
prayers entitled *Grateful Hearts Give Thanks*. It was a collection
of prayers from old to new, from the USA to other parts of the
world. We had mealtime prayers, bedtime prayers, prayers for
special occasions throughout the year. Each prayer focused on
how great God is and how we can return all of His blessings
to us by saying "Thank You."

When we individually and corporately can say "Thank You"
to God, we give witness to the world we are certainly aware
that all we have comes from above.

> This is the day the LORD has made. We will rejoice
> and be glad in it…Give thanks to the LORD, for he

is good! His faithful love endures forever (Psalm 118:24,29 NLT).

Lacking a thankful heart, we are self-centered, trying to acquire more and more, harsh with our words, and never satisfied with what we have; we need more and more. (A wise man once told me, "If you aren't satisfied with what you have, you will never be satisfied with what you want.") Malcontents are very rarely thankful for all they have. Enough is never enough. The world will give testimony to the fact that ingratitude leads to death and loss.

But when we have a thankful heart our lifestyle is changed. The password into God's presence is "Thank You." We read in Psalm 100:4,

> Enter His gates with thanksgiving and His courts
> with praise, give thanks to Him, bless His name.

Gratitude is how we enter into His presence. We must humble our hearts before approaching our good God. You can tell very easily what motivates another person by how he is able to give thanks for all that he has (see Romans 1:21). An ungodly man will not honor God or give thanks; he becomes futile in his speculations, and his foolish heart will be darkened.

> Give thanks in all circumstances, for this is God's
> will for you in Christ Jesus (1 Thessalonians 5:18
> NIV).

Spiritual thankfulness lets us say, "I don't need that." It will help us say no when we are tempted to purchase something that we would like, but don't have the money for. It will prevent us from having that rich chocolate dessert when we are trying to lose a few pounds and inches around our waistline. And sometimes in order to enforce the meaning behind "I don't need that" we may have to cut up some credit cards.

The thankful man will be content with all that God has provided. He will know that thankfulness is wanting what he has, not wanting more.[25]

Prayer

Father God, I can never say enough thanks to You. You have given me so many things to be thankful for. My cup is overflowing. Thank You, thank You. Amen.

Action

Take a risk and say, "Thank You" in God's presence.

Today's Wisdom

"For three things I thank God every day of my life: thanks that he has vouchsafed me knowledge of his works; deep thanks that he has set in my darkness the lamp of faith; deep, deepest thanks that I have another life to look forward to—a life joyous with light and flowers and heavenly song."

HELEN KELLER

Learn to Write on Stone

*A friend loves at all times, and a
brother is born for adversity.*

PROVERBS 17:17

Two friends were walking through the desert. At a certain point in the journey, they had an argument, and one slapped the other in the face.

The one who got slapped was hurt and speechless. He wrote in the sand: "Today my best friend slapped me in the face."

They kept on walking until they found an oasis, where they decided to take a swim in the water.

The one who got slapped started drowning, and the other saved him. When he recovered from the fright, he wrote on a stone, "Today my best friend saved my life."

The friend who had slapped and then saved his best friend asked him, "Why, after I hurt you, did you write in the sand—but now you write on a stone?"

The other friend, smiling, replied, "When a friend hurts us, we should write it down in the sand, where the winds of forgiveness are in charge of erasing it. When something great happens, we should engrave it in the stone of the memory of the heart, where no wind can erase it."[26]

This story makes me reflect on my own life. How do I write my friends' offenses against me: in sand or in stone? We need to major on the majors and minor on the minors. Let those minor offenses be written in sand where our memory lets the offenses be forgotten: However, when major events come into our lives they are to be written in stone where winds never blow them away.

I've been so fortunate in having some great "stone" friends. They are ones who stand by me during good times and bad times.

Friendships take time to develop. Men love to have side-by-side relationships. This is why they are attracted to other men who have like interests: golf, tennis, hiking, fishing, skiing, and so on. Women aren't always able to relate this aspect of their men to their understanding of friendship. They like friends to be able to sympathize with their inner emotions. Men like action, not words.

In order to have friends you have to be a friend. We have to assign top priority to our friendships. We must not wait for that friend to come to us; we must take the initiative. It isn't important to have too many friends, but as men we are to reach out and have those men in our lives who will hold us accountable to our beliefs.

Our style of dealing with other men is to attract, not cast off. Someone has well said, "The man who throws a stone at the birds scares them away, and the man who abuses a friend destroys a friendship."

Having friends is good for one's health and well-being. Those who have friends are usually happier than those who don't. Friends can be great encouragers. Treat them with great respect. They are rich resources for who you will be as a man.

Prayer

Father God, I thank You for giving me such great men friends. They enrich my life and give me great happiness. May we grasp more deeply the importance of having quality men as our friends. Amen.

 ## Action

Do something today for a friend that will be written on stone.

 ## Today's Wisdom

"Promises may get friends, but it is performance that must nurse and keep them."

OWEN FELTHAM (1624–1691)

Lord God,
You alone are the Great Healer.
When my mind and body are weak,
I look to You for strength
and reassurance.
Surround me each day
with the presence
of Your love and compassion.
Quiet my spirit,
so I may know Your goodness
and be filled with Your peace.
Heal me, Lord,
according to Your plan for my life.
This I pray through Jesus Christ,
my Lord. Amen.

Be Careful
What You Say

Death and life are in the power
of the tongue, and those who
love it will eat its fruit.

PROVERBS 18:21

The tongue is a very powerful tool in our lives. It can bring us death or it can bring us life. James gives a very strong warning about this power:

> Let everyone be quick to hear, slow to speak and slow to anger; for the anger of man does not achieve the righteousness of God (James 1:19-20).

Whether words give us death or life depends on how we choose them. We confirm and communicate with our wives by how we talk and how we listen.

We communicate in so many different ways. Often our looks and touches communicate as strongly as our words. These nonverbal signals transmit our feelings in a strong fashion. However, words are most often used. We desperately need to hear each other's voices tell us what we're thinking, how we're feeling, what we're dealing with, and what our dreams are.

How we put our thoughts into words will make a difference in whether our marriage is strong or weak, full of excitement or agony and pain, full of wellness or destruction. These times of conversation penetrate every aspect of our marriage. A key verse that guides us in this area is Ephesians 4:29:

> Let no unwholesome word proceed from your mouth, but only such a word as is good for edification according to the need of the moment that it may give grace to those who hear.

Communication is so very important to our healthy relationship with our mate. Therefore, we need to learn as much as possible how to develop this skill.

Listening is as valuable as speaking. If we are to have open communication, we must be vulnerable and honest, but we must also be good listeners. Don't be the kind of husband who waits for a break in your wife's words so you can jump in and give your opinion. When we are good listeners we allow the other person to be free to share without fear, rejection, or negative judgment. Good listening creates good bonding. The better we bond the closer we become. When a husband and wife are able to resolve their differences in a healthy fashion it permits them to disagree in the future in the same healthy way.

Recently, a reporter asked Billy Graham how he and his wife, Ruth, shared their intimacy together. Billy quickly replied, "We romance with our eyes!"

May we each learn to communicate with our eyes. Let your mate see you love her. Your eyes say, *You're special to me.* So put down the paper, turn off the TV, and give your full attention to what your wife is sharing.

Don't make the false assumption that your wife wants advice. Many times she just wants you to hear her out. When you're a good listener you are communicating to your wife that she's important to you.

Prayer

Father God, give me the desire to be a good communicator with my wife. Let me listen before I speak, and let my tongue be quiet till I know all the facts. Let me be attentive as we share ideas and thoughts. Amen.

 Action

Be quick to hear, slow to speak, and slow to anger.

 Today's Wisdom

"The two most important muscles which operate without the direction of the brain are the heart and the tongue."

ANONYMOUS

191

There's Always a "But"

*We know that God causes all things
to work together for good to those
who love God, to those who are
called according to His purpose.*

ROMANS 8:28

've noticed in Scripture that with every promise there is a
condition. In this key verse we read that all things do work
together for good. In our own family we believe that because
God says it and we have experienced it in our own lives. However, for this to be true we must meet a condition, that being
"to those who love God, to those who are called according to
His purpose."

The promise that "God causes all things to work together
for good" is reserved for the children of God. Sometimes this
promise is given to an unbeliever in order to give them comfort
during the death of a loved one, a bad failure in business, or
even a failed marriage. When we use this verse improperly it
may give comfort, but this promise is only for the believer who
has been chosen by God to be one of His children.

This verse is also a test of our loyalty to God. Are we only
fair-weather Christians? Or can we remain loyal to God even

during the difficult times of our lives? As Job was being tested by God, his wife asked him this question: "Do you still hold fast your integrity? Curse God and die!" Job's faithful response was classic: "Shall we indeed accept good from God and not accept adversity?" (Job 2:9-10).

Can we still see God's purpose for us in times of illness, death, lack of food, lack of work, lack of money, lack of home, and lack of family?

In our culture we're challenged to remain loyal to our work, our sports team, our country, our school, our spouse, our children—but seldom are we encouraged to remain loyal to God through all situations.

Larry Crabb reminded his readers in *The Marriage Builder* that the hope of the Christian lies not in a change of circumstances, which God may or may not bring about, but in the grace of God. We aren't to hope that the circumstances will change, but we are to hope in God's grace—in His unearned, undeserved, and unconditional love for us.

God promises to permit only those events to enter our lives that will further His purpose in our lives. Our responsibility is to respond to life's events in a way that will please the Lord, and not to try to change the circumstances into what we want.[27]

The idea is not that we work for God, but that because of our loyalty to Him He can work through us. Remember, God is the Potter and we are the clay. He wants to conform us to His own image, not our image. Since Americans live in a "now and feel-good" environment, this truth is hard to live out. We only want to do things that feel good right now. Many of life's character-building circumstances don't feel good. In fact, they often are quite painful. They are events we wouldn't choose for ourselves.

As a man, reaffirm your loyalty to God today. Acknowledge that He is God and that He permits only those events to come into our lives that are life-forming for us.

Prayer

Father God, I want to be loyal to You and trust that all things work together for good. This is a renewed trust. Give me the courage to live it out in my life. Amen.

 Action

Acknowledge that everything you have is on loan from God. He is the Potter and you are the clay. Let Him mold you in His own way.

 Today's Wisdom

"I will make up to you for the years that the swarming locust has eaten."

JOEL 2:25

Live on Solid Ground

*He will be the sure foundation for
your times, a rich store of salvation
and wisdom and knowledge; the fear of
the* Lord *is the key to this treasure.*

ISAIAH 33:6 NIV

Recently I received a letter from a dear friend we financially support in her ministry. She has expressed over the months that God has been guiding her in new ways but the path isn't clear yet. She sees changes on the horizon and isn't sure of what lies ahead, but her letter is a continuation of her search for new direction:

> At this point in my life I am facing changes in many respects, and if I did not know the Lord and if I did not know that He establishes and directs my steps, I could be shaken by some of what I see happening around me (Psalm 37:23; Proverbs 16:9).
>
> As I was thanking Him just a few days ago for the fact that I know He is the same yesterday, today, and forever (Hebrews 13:8) and that although circumstances and relationships may change, He never changes nor forsakes me (Hebrews 13:5), He

195

brought a verse to my mind that I have known over the years. Through this verse He has also brought comfort to me for these changing times I am in. The verse is Isaiah 33:6: "He shall be the stability of your times."

Isn't it a comfort to know truths that confirm His faithfulness to us, and then in addition to realize that He is our stability!

The word *stability* means the strength to stand or endure; firmness; the property of a body that causes it, when disturbed from a condition of equilibrium, to develop forces that restore the original condition.

What a promise! When we may feel shaken, He is firm and stands and endures for us! He is that which will always restore us to a condition of equilibrium, no matter what!

If you are not now in a situation in which changing circumstances are a factor, then you may not appreciate fully what this promise has meant to me in these last days, but you know a time will come when changes will be a factor and, as I said earlier, then you will want to embrace this truth. It will hold you with hope and confidence in a state of changes!

Thank you again for your faithfulness!

Here is one person who can recall and claim God's mighty Scriptures to see us through difficult times. Even though our stability is shaken in the present, He promises He will always be the same—never wavering.

Changes become a factor in all of our lives. If not today, then surely tomorrow or the next day. Isn't it wonderful to know that when changes come we can go to God's Word to find the strength to see us through another situation!

Let's not wait for the storm to seek verses that comfort and direct, but let's be prepared for when these days appear on the horizon (and they surely will) and have these fantastic truths in our memory bank.

 ## Prayer

Father God, I never know when these unstable situations will appear in my life. Let me prepare myself with Your Word, which will be an encouragement as I travel through these difficult times. Amen.

 ## Action

Read Psalm 37:23; Proverbs 16:9; Hebrews 13:8; Psalm 42:11.

 ## Today's Wisdom

"It is not a disgrace to fail. Failing is one of the greatest arts in the world."

Charles Kettering

We Are Called to Be Faithful

*I will sing of the lovingkindness of the
LORD forever, to all generations I will make
known Your faithfulness with my mouth.*

PSALM 89:1

I n all facets of life we hunger for people who will be faithful
to our many dimensions of life—in our marriage, with our
children, with our church, with our work, and with our business. When a person is faithful they will bring peace and
harmony to their lives and the lives of those around them.

In Deuteronomy 1 we see Moses revealing why God has
been faithful to him. After sharing how God has been faithful
in the past he goes on to say that...

- God is dependable—He does what He says (verses
  19-25).

- God is fair and just (verses 26-40).

- When we were fearful and doubted, God was fair
  and just (verses 26-40).

198

- When we were frustrated and overwhelmed, God was fair and just (verses 37-40).

- When we were arrogant and defiant, God was fair and just (verses 41-46).

He confirms this in Deuteronomy 7:9:

> Know therefore that the LORD your God, He is God, the faithful God, who keeps His covenant and His lovingkindness to a thousandth generation with those who love Him and keep His commandments.

Throughout Scripture we are challenged to be faithful men. We can be faithful to others because God is faithful to us. Here are some of the many ways He is faithful:

- *Promises.* "Faithful is He who calls you" (1 Thessalonians 5:24); "He who promised is faithful" (Hebrews 10:23).

- *Power.* "[God] does not become weary or tired" (Isaiah 40:28).

- *Character.* "If we are faithless, He remains faithful, for He cannot deny Himself" (2 Timothy 2:13).

- *Protection.* "The Lord is faithful, and He will strengthen and protect you from the evil one" (2 Thessalonians 3:3).

- *Provision.* "Just as I have been with Moses, I will be with you; I will not fail you or forsake you" (Joshua 1:5).

- *Temptation.* "No temptation has overtaken you but such as is common to man; and God is faithful, who will not allow you to be tempted beyond what you are able, but with the temptation will provide the way of escape also, that you may be able to endure it" (1 Corinthians 10:13).

- *Forgiveness.* "If we confess our sins, He is faithful and righteous to forgive us our sins and to cleanse us from all unrighteousness" (1 John 1:9).

- *Love.* "God is faithful, through whom you were called into fellowship with His Son, Jesus Christ our Lord" (1 Corinthians 1:9).

- *Hope.* "I still dare to hope when I remember this: The unfailing love of the LORD never ends! By his mercies we have been kept from complete destruction. Great is his faithfulness; his mercies begin afresh each day" (Lamentations 3:21-23 NLT).

Faithfulness is a "God thing." How faithful we are as men will determine our destiny. God has been faithful in the past, He is in the present, and He will be in the future. Because God is faithful, we can also be faithful in every situation of life. No wonder God is looking for faithful men.

 Prayer

Father God, grant me the desire to be faithful to You. Your Word has made me realize that faithfulness is a great character trait. Give me strength to make daily decisions that will give me life, not death. Because You are faithful You give me hope for the future. Amen.

 Action

ACTION

Read chapter 1 of Deuteronomy to see how Moses realized God's faithfulness to the Israelites.

Today's Wisdom

"I've been driven many times to my knees by the over-whelming conviction that I had nowhere else to go."

ABRAHAM LINCOLN

We All Have Traps

No temptation has overtaken you but such as is common to man; and God is faithful, who will not allow you to be tempted beyond what you are able, but with the temptation will provide the way of escape also, that you may be able to endure it.

1 CORINTHIANS 10:13

recently read the following interesting story:

> If you put a buzzard in a pen six or eight feet square and entirely open at the top, the bird, in spite of his ability to fly, will be an absolute prisoner. The reason is that a buzzard always begins a flight from the ground with a run of ten or twelve feet. Without space to run, as is his habit, he will not even attempt to fly, but will remain a prisoner for life in a small jail with no top.
>
> The ordinary bat that flies around at night, a remarkably nimble creature in the air, cannot take off from a level place. If it is placed on the floor or flat ground, all it can do is shuffle about helplessly and, no doubt, painfully, until it reaches some slight elevation from which it can throw itself into the air. Then, at once, it takes off like a flash.

A bumblebee, if dropped into an open tumbler, will be there until it dies unless it is taken out. It never sees the means of escape at the top, but persists in trying to find some way out through the sides near the bottom. It will seek a way where none exists, until it completely destroys itself.[28]

In many ways, there are a lot of us like the buzzard, the bat, and the bee. We are struggling about with all our problems and frustrations, not realizing that if we look up, we'll find the answer.

We must ask the basic question, "What is my trap?" We all have them. Some are more severe than others, but we find ourselves not being the man God wants us to be. We try this, we try that; we turn to the right, we turn to the left; we join this club, we join that group. Nothing seems to give us the peace we are looking for. When this happens it's time to look up!

The thief comes only to steal and kill and destroy; I came that they might have life, and have it abundantly (John 10:10).

A few years ago our local police chief started coming to our early morning Bible study. He hadn't had very many experiences with Christian men before and didn't know what to expect. He was very faithful in his attendance at that early hour. He even ventured out to our men's retreat. After driving back down the mountain from our retreat he said, "I didn't know you could have so much fun being a Christian." His trap was that he had never been exposed to men who knew how to live abundantly. Maybe you are living in the same box—your trap is keeping you from the abundant life.

We have to learn to think out of the box. Think beyond our experience. Don't let your past prevent you from experiencing the blessings of the future. Stop holding back from attending that church, that men's study, that men's retreat. You may have good reasons for not going, but go anyhow. There are men in your life who are challenging you to look up and you have been reluctant in doing so. Take a risk and go. Jump out of your trap—whatever it is.

 ## Prayer

Father God, I've looked down, around, and below, and nothing seems to satisfy me. For a change, I want to look up. Please give me the courage to get out of my dead-end box. With Your help I will. Amen.

 ## Action

Get out of your trap. Write down how you plan on doing that, so you have it in front of you every morning. Then, follow through.

 ## Today's Wisdom

"Since habits become power, make them work with you and not against you."

E. STANLEY JONES

This is what the L ORD says: "Cursed is the one who trusts in man, who depends on flesh for his strength and whose heart turns away from the L ORD. He will be like a bush in the wastelands; he will not see prosperity when it comes. He will dwell in the parched places of the desert, in a salt land where no one lives.

"But blessed is the man who trusts in the L ORD, whose confidence is in him. He will be like a tree planted by the water that sends out its roots by the stream. It does not fear when heat comes; its leaves are always green. It has no worries in a year of drought and never fails to bear fruit."

JEREMIAH 17:5-8 NIV

Come Clean with God

*It is a trustworthy statement, deserving
full acceptance, that Christ Jesus
came into the world to save sinners,
among whom I am foremost of all.*

1 TIMOTHY 1:15

Currently, one of the most watched TV programs is Donald Trump's *Celebrity Apprentice*. For many, the highlight of the program is when Mr. Trump shows his delight in saying, "You're fired!"

As men, we never want to hear our boss utter, "You're fired!" But if that happens, it's only a human boss ending our current employment. On the other hand, Jesus says to us, "You're hired!" Jesus hires us to work for Him and gives us all the necessary tools to do a great job. Plus, working for Him, we have permanent job security.

But in order for us to be hired we must first humble ourselves and come clean with God. The apostle Paul had to do this when he was confronted by this man called Jesus Christ. He looked back to this in his writings:

- "I am the worst sinner of all" (1 Timothy 1:15).

- "I am the least of all the apostles" (1 Corinthians 15:9).
- "I am the least deserving Christian there is" (Ephesians 3:8).

Paul was humbled and wanted to change his direction.

At one time in my life I had to make a decision. Old things had to pass away, and I had to turn to eternal values, not to those which would go up in smoke. My cry was, "How do I come close to you, God?"

The answer came from His Word:

> Here are my directions: Pray much for others; plead for God's mercy upon them; give thanks for all he is going to do for them. Pray in this way for kings and all others who are in authority over us, or are in places of high responsibility, so that we can live in peace and quietness, spending our time in godly living and thinking much about the Lord. This is good and pleases God our Savior, for he longs for all to be saved and to understand this truth (1 Timothy 2:1-4 TLB).

Three things are evident from Paul's challenge to Timothy (and to us):

- pray for your needs
- pray for others
- pray for thanksgiving

Notice that we are to go from the inside of ourselves to the outside of others. We are a very narcissistic society. We love to look in the mirror to see how good we look. We see a group photograph we're in and look first for ourselves. But when God hires us to work for Him, it's in our job description that we're to use our energies to help others.

Getting ahead is what Donald Trump's show is all about. But it takes the normal worldly course, which says to get ahead is to go *up* the ladder of success. But with God, the way to a promotion is to become humble…to allow ourselves to become of less importance.

May God grant us the ability to be men who are humble… and willing to come clean with Him—all the time.

Prayer

Father God, help me to come clean. Let me very objectively realize that my present life doesn't fill my purpose. Give me the courage to realize I've been wrong in the past. I want Your solution for my future. Amen.

Action

Come clean with those you love most—your family.

Today's Wisdom

"One of the best legacies a father can leave his children is to love their mother."

C. NEIL STRAIT

Reflect Hope

*Now faith is the assurance of things hoped for,
the conviction of things not seen.*

HEBREWS 11:1

As leaders of our homes we must assure those around us that we are marching to the tune of hope. Hope is what makes us excited for each sunrise. We can't wait to get started. Hope makes us the cheerleader for all those around us.

Many of the people in our country no longer have hope. They have either lost or never found the reason for hope. Our young people find little to get excited about or are pessimistically not looking forward to the future. When this happens it is a sign that there is no hope in their lives. True, godly hope does not disappoint, however:

> A terminal disease seized the eldest son and heir of the Duke of Hamilton. A little before he passed away he took his Bible from under his pillow and opened it at the passage, "I have fought a good fight, I have finished my course, I have kept the faith: henceforth there is laid up for me a crown of

209

righteousness, which the Lord, the righteous Judge, shall give me at that day: and not to me only, but unto them also that love his appearing." As death approached, he called his younger brother to his bedside, and addressing him with the greatest affection and seriousness, closed with these remarkable words: "And now, Douglas, in a little time you'll be a duke, but I shall be a king."[29]

Here is a young man who had his hope based upon the promises of God. What is your hope based upon? The economy, your wealth, your possessions, your titles? All of these can go south with the smallest downturn in the world's economy.

Nothing is forever. It's much more secure to base your hope and trust on things that are eternal—those treasures that will never fade away, because they are backed by a promissory note notarized by God. These promises were true when written and are still true today. This kind of hope is neither Republican nor Democrat; it makes no difference who is in the White House.

As heads of our families, we are to give hope to each individual under our umbrella of responsibility. When we fulfill this duty, we become a cheerleader for the future. We don't have to give hype or empty promises. We must let those around know that no matter what the situation there is hope. False hope disappoints, but hope based upon God's Word can give definite direction toward our future.

Look back and review in Scripture what God has done before our time. This will give you hope during our time. God is the same today as He was in the past, and He will be the same for the future.

Prayer

Father God, as the man of the house I want to be known as a man of *hope*. When others get down I want to look up. I want to be known as a husband and father who puts his faith in Your Word. You are able to keep and protect in all situations. May Your will be done in my life. Amen.

 Action

Where do you need hope today? Go to Scripture and see what God has to say on the situation.

 Today's Wisdom

TWELVE REASONS TO HAVE HOPE

1. God understands you and your problems (Matthew 6:8).

2. God proved His love at the cross (Romans 8:32).

3. God loves you as His child (Romans 8:15-16).

4. God's power is available to you (Philippians 4:13).

5. God promises to supply all your needs (Philippians 4:19).

6. God can exceed your highest expectations (Ephesians 3:20).

7. God uses trials to display your faith (Philippians 2:15).

8. God works all things together for good (Romans 8:28).

9. God's will is good, acceptable, and perfect (Romans 12:2).

10. God's grace is sufficient for you (2 Corinthians 12:9).

11. God uses trials to produce maturity (James 1:2-4).

12. God is always with you (Hebrews 13:5).[30]

Offerings in Righteousness

He will sit as a smelter and
purifier of silver.

MALACHI 3:3

Have you ever wondered when you will be complete in
God's eyes? How many times do you have to go to
church, how much money do you have to give, how much
time do you have to spend reading Scripture and praying in
order for you to be righteous? All Christians at one time or
another ask this question. Why? Because we live in a culture
that rewards people according to their works—not on who they
are, but on what they do. That's why Paul gave us Ephesians
2:8-9: "By grace you have been saved through faith; and not
of yourselves, it is the gift of God not as a result of works, so
that no one should boast."

Here's a story that confirms this.

> Many years ago, a few ladies met in a certain city
> to read the Scriptures and make them the sub-
> ject of conversation. While in the third chapter of
> Malachi, they came upon a remarkable expression

in the third verse: "And he shall sit as a refiner and purifier of silver."

One lady's opinion was that it was intended to convey the view of the sanctifying influence of the grace of Christ. Then she proposed to visit a silversmith and report to them what he said on the subject. She went accordingly and without telling the object of her errand, begged to know the process of refining silver, which he fully described to her.

"But sir," she said, "do you sit while the work of refining is going on?"

"Oh, yes, madam," replied the silversmith; "I must sit with my eye steadily fixed on the furnace, for if the time necessary for refining be exceeded in the slightest degree, the silver will be injured."

The lady at once saw the beauty, and comfort too, of the expression, "He shall sit as a refiner and purifier of silver." Christ sees it needful to put His children into a furnace; but His eye is steadily intent on the work of purifying, and His wisdom and love are both engaged in the best manner for them. Their trials do not come at random; and they are only as intense and last only as long as is necessary for the refining process; "the very hairs of your head are all numbered."

As the lady was preparing to leave the shop, the silversmith concluded by saying that he knew the process of purifying was complete when he could see his own image reflected in the silver.[31]

What a beautiful example! When Christ sees His own image in His people, His work of purifying is accomplished. As I examine my own life I can readily see that God has not purified me to the point where He can be seen at all times in my life. I must have some more intense heat of purification before I am righteous. However, my hope is that I will be and am righteous in Jesus.

In the future there is laid up for me the crown of righteousness, which the Lord, the righteous Judge, will award to me on that day; and not only to me, but also to all who have loved His appearing (2 Timothy 4:8).

Prayer

Father God, what a beautiful comparison of the purification of silver and my own purification. May my life be a continuous growth toward a righteous life. Assist me on my journey. Amen.

Action

Be encouraged to be a man of God, realizing that all of life's experiences are a process of purification.

Today's Wisdom

"Please be patient with me, God isn't finished with me yet!"

BILL GOTHARD

Do not fear, for I am with you;
do not anxiously look about
you, for I am your God.

I will strengthen you, surely
I will help you,

surely I will uphold you with
my righteous right hand.

ISAIAH 41:10

My Utmost
for His Highest

If you...being evil, know how to give
good gifts to your children, how much
more shall your heavenly Father give the
Holy Spirit to those who ask Him?

LUKE 11:13

This verse had a great impact on the life of one of the great Christian writers, Oswald Chambers. Chambers, who came to know Jesus by the teaching of the great Charles Spurgeon, never lived to see the popularity of the book that would bear his name, the classic daily devotional *My Utmost for His Highest.*

At his conversion Oswald Chambers claimed God's promise that the Holy Spirit had been given to him, as stated in today's verse. He testified he had no vision of heaven or angels. He was dry and empty, no power or realization of God. Then he was asked to speak at a meeting, and in response, 40 souls came forward to the front of the church to commit their lives to Christ. From that day on he found power and peace in ministry that impacted the world both during and after his life.

But tragically, Chambers died suddenly in Egypt on November 15, 1917, while serving British troops during World

War I. He was buried in Cairo under a headstone bearing the words of Luke 11:13. Only later did his widow, Gertrude Hobbs, compile his manuscripts, notes, lectures, and sermons into *My Utmost for His Highest*, which is still the most popular devotional among Christians around the world.

Here was a man who was searching for more authority and power for his writing and speaking. Not until he learned about this part of the Trinity called the Holy Spirit did he realize his power for service in the Christian life.

Charles Ryrie comments about Luke 11:13 that "since the day of Pentecost the gift of the Spirit is given to all believers."[32] Maybe you find yourself dried out, burned out, with no power in your Christian walk. You scratch your head and want to know where that first love has gone. Yes, we all can be living a powerless life, as Oswald Chambers was until he was touched by the reality of Luke 11:13.

If this is the cure, then claim what God says to be true: As believers we have the power and might of the third part of the Trinity—the Holy Spirit. Receive from God all the privileges that go with the indwelling of the Holy Spirit. Study the Word and see the wonderful truths God reveals to us about the relationship between the Holy Spirit and the believer.

 Prayer

Father God, I come to You wanting more of the experience with the Holy Spirit that Oswald Chambers had. Awaken my soul that I might claim what has already been given to me. I want to exhibit power in my beliefs and not be timid in my unbelief. Amen.

Action

Claim all the provisions that come with possessing the Holy Spirit in your life.

Today's Wisdom

"Without the presence of the Spirit there is no conviction, no regeneration, no sanctification, no cleansing, no acceptable works. We can perform duties without him, but our service is dull and mechanical. Life is in the quickening Spirit."

W.A. CRISWELL

Notes

1. Found on the Internet. Author unknown.

2. Adapted from Bob Barnes, *15 Minutes Alone with God* (Eugene, OR: Harvest House Publishers, 1995), pp. 12-15.

3. Adapted from Bob and Emilie Barnes, *15-Minute Devotions for Couples* (Eugene, OR: Harvest House Publishers, 1995), pp. 169-173.

4. Found on the Internet. Author unknown.

5. Adapted from Chad Merrihew (my grandson), essay written for his application to the University of Oregon in Eugene, Oregon, June 2003. Used by permission.

6. This story has been circulated as true, but no such event actually occurred. (See www.truthorfiction.com/rumors/m/motherbird.htm.)

7. Taken from a personal letter sent by a friend.

8. Adapted from Emilie Barnes, *More Faith in My Day* (Eugene, OR: Harvest House Publishers, 2005), pp. 183-184.

9. Found on the Internet. Author unknown.

10. Story used by permission of Dennis E. Hensley. Copyright 1967, renewed 1991.

11. Oswald Chambers, *My Utmost for His Highest* (Westwood, NJ: Barbour and Company, Inc., n.d.), p. 50.

12. *Treasury of God's Virtues*, Elaine Wright Colvin and Elaine Cressman, eds. (Lincolnwood, IL: Publications International, Ltd., 1999), p. 246.

13. Jenny Whitney, from a letter she sent me on Father's Day 2002. Used by permission.

14. Adapted from Barnes, *15-Minute Devotions for Couples*, pp. 11-13.

15. *Health-Life Report*, Health-Life American Association (Little Rock, AR), vol. 7, number 2.

16. Author unknown. Found on the Internet.

17. Charles C. Ryrie, *The Ryrie Study Bible* (Chicago: Moody Press, 1973), p. 968.

18. Author unknown. Found on the Internet. Variously associated with the names "Brian A. 'Drew' Chalker" and "Rob McBeth."

19. The Tract League, Grand Rapids, MI, #185.

20. Robert J. Morgan, *Then Sings My Soul* (Nashville, TN: Thomas Nelson, Inc., 2003), p. 261.

21. Adapted from Bob and Emilie Barnes, *Minute Meditations on Prayer* (Eugene, OR: Harvest House Publishers, 2003), pp. 88-89.

22. Author unknown.

23. Adapted from Robert D. Foster, *Seven Minutes with God* (Colorado Springs, CO: NavPress, 1997), from a tract titled "How to Plan a Daily Quiet Time."

24. Rick Warren, *The Purpose-Driven Life* (Grand Rapids, MI: Zondervan, 2002), p. 7.

25. Adapted from Kenton Beshore, Thanksgiving Day message, Mariners Church, Irvine, CA, November 2004.

26. Adapted from Joe Gatuslao, *Good News Journal*, vol. IV, number 1, 2002 (Leander, TX), p. 18.

27. Larry Crabb, *The Marriage Builder* (Grand Rapids, MI: Zondervan, 1982), pp. 105-106.

28. Author unknown. Found on the Internet.

29. Source unknown.

30. Taken from Dale Burke, *Less Is More Leadership* (Eugene, OR: Harvest House Publishers, 2004), pp. 222-223.

31. Author unknown. Adapted.

32. Ryrie, p. 1568, Luke 11:13 footnote.

Harvest House Books by Bob & Emilie Barnes

Bob & Emilie Barnes

*15-Minute Devotions
for Couples*
Good Manners for Today's Kids
*Simple Secrets Couples
Should Know*
Together Moments for Couples

Bob Barnes

5-Minute Bible Workouts for Men
*15 Minutes Alone
with God for Men*
Five Minutes in the Bible for Men
*What Makes a Man
Feel Loved*

Emilie Barnes

15 Minutes Alone with God
*15 Minutes of Peace
with God*
*15 Minutes with God
for Grandma*
101 Ways to Love Your Grandkids
*365 Things Every Woman
Should Know*
*500 Time-Saving Hints
for Every Woman*

Friendship Teas to Go
Good Manners in Minutes
*A Grandma Is a Gift
from God*
Heal My Heart, Lord
If Teacups Could Talk
In the Stillness of Quiet Moments
An Invitation to Tea
Journey through Cancer
Let's Have a Tea Party!
A Little Book of Manners
A Little Princess in the Making
The Little Teacup that Talked
*Minute Meditations for
Busy Moms*
*Minute Meditations for Healing
and Hope*
More Faith in My Day
More Hours in My Day
*Quiet Moments Alone
with God*
The Twelve Teas® of Inspiration
Walk with Me Today, Lord
Youniquely Woman

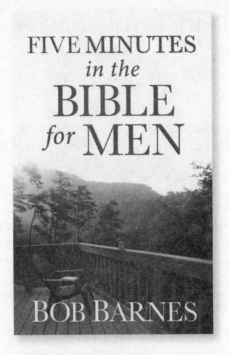

FIVE MINUTES
in the
BIBLE
for MEN

BOB BARNES

Take Five...
and Come Alive in Faith

We all need the encouragement and accountability of other men.
Bestselling author Bob Barnes invites you to spend five minutes
a day in devotions exploring the riches of God's Word. Whether
you take your five in the morning, evening, or in between meet-
ings, those few minutes offer

- compelling stories and illustrations of strength and
  faithfulness
- connection to the inspirational lives of godly men
- God's truths and promises for your personal path

This focused time will draw you to God's presence and lead you
to embrace a faith that transforms your life and inspires the lives
of others.